NO BETTER
FRIEND

★ ★

NO BETTER FRIEND

A MAN, A DOG, AND THEIR INCREDIBLE TRUE STORY OF FRIENDSHIP AND SURVIVAL IN WORLD WAR II

★ ROBERT WEINTRAUB ★

YOUNG READERS EDITION

LITTLE, BROWN AND COMPANY
New York   Boston

No Better Friend: Young Readers Edition was adapted by Robert Weintraub for young readers. It is an abridgment of *No Better Friend* by Robert Weintraub, published by Little, Brown and Company.

Little, Brown and Company

Hachette Book Group
1290 Avenue of the Americas, New York, NY 10104
Visit us at lb-kids.com

Little, Brown and Company is a division of Hachette Book Group, Inc.
The Little, Brown name and logo are trademarks of Hachette Book Group, Inc.

The publisher is not responsible for websites (or their content) that are not owned by the publisher.

First Edition: May 2016

Maps by David Lambert

Library of Congress Cataloging-in-Publication Data

Names: Weintraub, Robert.
Title: No better friend : young readers edition : a man, a dog, and their incredible true story of friendship and survival in World War II / Robert Weintraub.
Description: First edition. | New York, NY : Little, Brown and Company, 2016.
Identifiers: LCCN 2016002795 | ISBN 9780316344678 (hardcover) | ISBN 9780316344661 (ebook) | ISBN 9780316344647 (library edition ebook)
Subjects: LCSH: Judy (Dog), 1936–1950—Juvenile literature. | Dogs—War use—Juvenile literature. | World War, 1939–1945—Prisoners and prisons, Japanese—Juvenile literature. | Prisoners of war—Great Britain—Juvenile literature. | Prisoners of war—Pacific Area—Juvenile literature. | Great Britain. Royal Navy—Mascots—Juvenile literature. | Williams, Frank, 1919–2003—Biography—Juvenile literature. | Sailors—Great Britain—Biography—Juvenile literature. | Human-animal relationships—Juvenile literature.
Classification: LCC D810.A65 W452 2016 | DDC 940.54/72520929—dc23
LC record available at http://lccn.loc.gov/2016002795

10 9 8 7 6 5 4 3

LSC-C

Printed in the United States of America

For my children, Phoebe and Marty

Courage is not having the strength to go on; it is going on when you don't have the strength.

—*Theodore Roosevelt*

CONTENTS

Prologue   *1*

Chapter 1: Frank and Judy   5

   The Sino-Japanese War   *8*

   World War Two   *13*

Chapter 2: Singapore   16

   The Battle of Britain   *17*

   Pearl Harbor   *18*

Chapter 3: Flight   23

Chapter 4: Attack   26

Chapter 5: Frank's Escape   33

Chapter 6: Saving Judy   40

Chapter 7: Posic Island   46

Chapter 8: Pompong   52

Chapter 9: Jungle Trek   57

Chapter 10: Padang   67

Chapter 11: Meeting the Enemy   73

General Chiang Kai-shek   *76*

The Geneva Conventions   *77*

Chapter 12: Captives   79

Chapter 13: Prison   84

Chapter 14: On the Move   91

The Allied Powers and the Axis Powers   *96*

Chapter 15: Gloegoer   98

Chapter 16: Hungry and Tired   104

Chapter 17: Judy and the Skull   111

Chapter 18: Judy Meets Frank   116

Chapter 19: Best Friends   120

Chapter 20: POW #81-A   126

Chapter 21: Nishi   135

Chapter 22: Sneaking Aboard   145

Chapter 23: Hell Ship   149

Knots and Bells   *156*

Chapter 24: Rescue Dog   168

Chapter 25: River Valley   173

Chapter 26: A New Home in the Jungle   182

Chapter 27: Dangers   192

Chapter 28: Escapes   200

Chapter 29: Dark Thoughts   206

V-J Day/Atomic Bombs   *215*

Chapter 30: Going Home   218

Chapter 31: Quarantine   224

Chapter 32: David   227
   D-Day   *230*
Chapter 33: Recovery   234
Chapter 34: Heroes   241
   War Dogs   *248*
Chapter 35: Portsmouth   253
   PTSD   *257*
Chapter 36: Africa   259
Chapter 37: Judy Disappears   267
Chapter 38: Memorial   273
Epilogue   278
Timeline   282
Bibliography   285
Acknowledgments   289

PROLOGUE

The dog watched from the shadows of the jungle.

Something was about to happen. Something bad.

The dog, a female, could always sense these moments.
A powerful nose could detect human emotions very clearly.
Anger and fear were coming in strong waves from the
clearing a few hundred feet away.

These were common emotions in this forgotten corner
of World War Two, and the dog sensed them a lot. The dog
was, incredibly enough, an official prisoner of war, and
had lived with POWs held by the Japanese Army for years.

There had been close scrapes along the way. The dog
was constantly hiding from the guards, zipping in and out

of trouble. Usually, the dog's best friend, another prisoner, would call, or whistle, or snap his fingers. Then the dog would know when to move.

But not this time.

A guard in a gray-green uniform was screaming. He held a weapon often used by these enraged men. It was a long stick, one just like those the dog often chewed on in the forest. A man was cowering on the ground, waiting for the blows from the screaming guard to rain down on his head and body.

Then the guard started to beat the man with the stick.

It was time for action.

The dog raced out of the bush, barking like crazy. The guard was startled. He backed away from the beaten man, who lay on the ground, helpless.

The dog forced herself between the guard and the scared man. When the dog was sure the guard was watching her, she moved away. The guard followed, forgetting about the man on the ground.

He put the stick down and picked up another weapon, something long and thin. The dog knew what this was. It was also used to threaten, and to hurt. Many times before, angry men had fired something at her from this loud, dangerous device.

It was time to run.

The dog heard her best friend shout, "Judy, disappear!" The dog didn't turn to look, just jumped for the cover of the trees.

Then another sound—the weapon being used.

The dog felt the heat, and the sting.

She disappeared into the shadows once more.

Her best friend watched, breathing heavily, shocked and silent.

Was Judy alive—or dead?

FRANK AND JUDY

World War Two would bring them together, but it took a while before Frank Williams met Judy, the dog who would become his best friend.

They came of age a world apart. Judy was born in 1936 in Shanghai, China, in a kennel for dogs belonging to British citizens. When she was just a few weeks old, Judy escaped from her outdoor pen to run free in the busy, dangerous city. She wasn't ready to be on her own when she was so young and delicate. She nearly starved, but a kindly shopkeeper provided her with enough food to survive. One day, some Japanese sailors entered the store. There was an argument, and the sailors beat up the old shop owner. Judy came in to investigate, and one of the Japanese men kicked her across the street.

This turned out to be a lucky break for the young English pointer, for she was discovered shortly afterward, shivering in a doorway, by a girl who worked at Judy's kennel. The girl brought the pup back for a warm bath and a large supper. She also gave the dog a name, calling her *shudi*, which meant "peaceful one" in the local Chinese dialect. The head of the kennel, a British woman, changed this to "Judy."

Within a few weeks, Judy was adopted. Most dogs in the kennel were placed in local homes, but Judy's new home was a boat—a warship, actually. England kept a small part of its Royal Navy in China, and a fleet of small, maneuverable gunboats sailed on the Yangtze River, the largest river in the country and the third longest in the world. The gunboats protected British commercial interests in the area, fighting local pirates and warlords when they threatened Western trade.

Judy was taken in by the sailors aboard one of these gunboats, HMS *Gnat*. She was meant to be the ship's mascot but quickly proved to be more than that. Her barks provided warnings when pirates approached, and she showed an uncanny ability to sense when aircraft were nearby.

Judy's first true home, the Yangtze River gunboat HMS Gnat.

This proved especially useful when war broke out between China and Japan in 1937 (see sidebar). While the British were officially neutral, all Western ships, including American boats, were harassed and occasionally attacked by Japanese planes. Judy howled, barked, and generally made a racket when she detected a plane in the area. The gunboat crew knew what that meant—get to the guns, pronto!

THE SINO-JAPANESE WAR

China and Japan are two of Asia's largest countries and have a long history of fighting each other. In 1937, while Judy was serving with the gunboat fleet on the Yangtze River, Japan invaded China, kicking off the Sino-Japanese War (*Sino* means "Chinese," much like *Anglo* means "English").

Japan is much smaller than China and needs to get food and important materials from other countries. Japan often looked to China to supply these goods, sometimes taking them by force. In addition to needing a steady stream of supplies from China, Japan wanted to create an empire much the way Great Britain had done, by ruling other countries. China was a natural place to start, since the country was so huge that it was hard to defend and govern. Japan sent forces to the northern part of China, called Manchuria, and became friendly with the warlords in charge of the region. Japan received food and other goods in return.

But that wasn't enough. So next, Japan invaded the main part of China. Japan claimed that its soldiers were fired upon by Chinese forces near Beijing at a place called the Marco Polo Bridge. In response, Japan sent its soldiers into China, and Japan's air force began bombing China's cities.

At first, the Japanese easily took territory, but the Chinese fought much harder than anyone thought they would. Japan had a more modern army, but China had the advantage of fighting on its own territory. The war was very brutal, as the Japanese killed many thousands of civilians living in big Chinese cities, and eventually settled into a stalemate when it was clear neither side could fully win.

Then World War Two began, and Japan looked for the goods it wanted from other countries in Asia. The fighting in China mostly quieted as Japan fought in many other places.

Judy shows she can follow orders as well as any sailor.

Time and again, Judy surely saved the boat with her warnings. Once, though, she herself needed rescue. Early in her time aboard the *Gnat*, she fell overboard. The Yangtze River is muddy and fast-running, and Judy wasn't a natural swimmer. Fortunately, a sailor immediately yelled, "Man overboard!" (Wrong species, right spirit.) A motorboat was sent out to fetch Judy before she could drown.

If that was the lowlight of Judy's time in China, the highlight was the birth of her puppies. She became enamored of another English pointer, named Paul, who was aboard a French gunboat on the Yangtze. Shortly afterward, Judy became a mother. She gave birth to a litter of ten puppies, who soon swarmed the ship on their chubby little legs, gnawing on slipcovers, ammo belts, canvas sails, and everything else that wasn't metal. They also left puddles all over the boat. Because of the trouble they caused, the pups were given away, mostly to lucky local families.

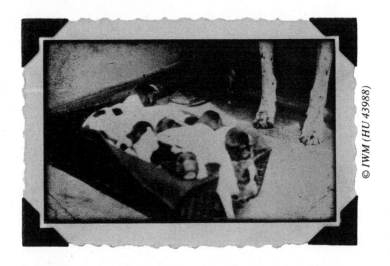

© IWM (HU 43988)

Judy's first litter, born in 1938, contained ten pups who lived. The father was another pointer, named Paul. The mother's legs are in the background.

Several of Judy's pups take a stroll on the ship's deck.

Judy met many of these locals when she headed ashore with her crew mates. A favorite canteen offered a delicious assortment of ice cream, and Judy quickly learned to love the sweet stuff, always begging for a bowlful. Once, her plaintive whines went unanswered, so she ambled behind the bar and pulled out a large carton of vanilla, which she dragged into the center of the room. After that, she always received her scoop in short order. She also ambled along with her crew mates on exercise runs and played soccer and field hockey with them. She would play on both teams in hockey, dashing in to grab the ball and deposit it in whichever goal struck her fancy. When the game ended, the sailors subtracted Judy's "goals" from the total score to determine the winner.

One thing she never did, however, was "point"—the very hunting aid she was bred to perform. She couldn't grasp the method of standing stiffly and staring toward birds in the bushes so that the crew could shoot them for dinner, but she was great at alerting her friends to danger.

© IWM (HU 439871)

Thanks to her friendly manner and ability to warn the ship of impending danger, Judy became a treasured member of the crew.

Judy would happily have gone on living a fulfilling life in China, but the threat of world war (see sidebar) was gathering, and she was, after all, in the service of the Royal Navy. First, she was transferred to a new gunboat, HMS *Grasshopper*, which was bigger and faster than the *Gnat*. She followed along as the *Grasshopper* was transferred out of China to Singapore, site of Britain's largest naval base in the Pacific.

WORLD WAR TWO

The Second World War began on September 1, 1939, a little more than two decades after the First World War ended in 1918. Germany was on the losing end of that first war, and the resulting loss of prestige and economic might led to the rise of the Nazi Party, with Adolph Hitler as its leader. Hitler quickly rebuilt the German military and began a policy of expansion. After taking over a few surrounding areas, including Austria and part of Czechoslovakia, Hitler's invasion of Poland in 1939 was the final straw for France and England, the principal nations opposing Germany. They declared war, beginning what would become nearly six years of war in Europe, eventually drawing in the United States, before Hitler and the Nazis were at last defeated.

World War II in the Pacific began later, in 1941, as the result of the Japanese attack on Pearl Harbor (see sidebar page 17). Much like the Germans, the Japanese had upset the balance of power in the region by aggressively expanding its empire. For several years, war was conducted by economic means—America cut off sales of oil and other important materials to Japan, which only made the small island nation more desperate to procure natural resources.

Frank Williams wound up in Singapore as well, though he wouldn't meet his future best friend in the Lion City. He grew up in the seaside town of Portsmouth, England. Frank was born in 1919; his father died when Frank was young. Frank and his five brothers and sisters (he was the second oldest) shared a small house with another family, a crowded situation Frank did his best to escape as often as possible. When he was a kid, this meant tooling around town on his bicycle, but once he turned sixteen, Frank joined the merchant navy (the British version of the American merchant marine), working on a ship as it carried supplies around the world. A few years later, with war threatening Europe, Frank joined the Royal Air Force (RAF). He loved flying and airplanes, but alas, he was too tall to be a pilot. Instead, he became a mechanic, specializing in radar systems, which at the time represented a brand-new, vital technology that would allow Frank and other "radarmen" to detect the presence of enemy aircraft in time to prepare for an attack.

HMS Grasshopper *was an upgraded gunboat that replaced the* Gnat *to become Judy's new home in 1938.*

Frank arrived in Singapore with a new, top secret radar unit in the summer of 1941.

SINGAPORE

Judy spent the months before the start of the Pacific war (the war was already well under way in Europe by now) performing routine patrol duties aboard the *Grasshopper* and relaxing in the homes of local officials in the Singapore government and military.

Frank's radar unit didn't have it so good. Immediately, problems cropped up. Equipment failed, and replacement parts were hard to come by. The ancient planes they had to work with, far less modern than the RAF aircraft that had won the Battle of Britain (see sidebar), weren't up to snuff. But there was no fighting yet, and the men enjoyed Singapore greatly.

On December 7, 1941, that changed drastically. The Japanese attacked the US Navy base at Pearl Harbor in Hawaii (see sidebar). It was part of a broader wave of invasions across the Pacific by the Japanese, one that included Siam (now Thailand) and Malaya (now Malaysia). Both nations were close to Singapore, the center of strength for the British Empire in Asia. The island had a huge military presence, including the large naval base, and it was considered invulnerable. Certainly, few there were concerned about the Japanese.

PEARL HARBOR

On December 7, 1941, the Japanese military unleashed a shocking surprise attack on the huge US naval base at Pearl Harbor, on the Hawaiian island of Oahu. The blow led directly to America's declaring war and entering World War Two.

The operation began when the Japanese Navy sent aircraft carriers within striking distance of Pearl. At dawn on a Sunday morning, more than 350 planes attacked the base, dropping bombs and firing machine guns at the American ships docked there. Most of Pearl was still asleep when the attack came.

More than 2,400 people were killed and over 1,100 wounded.

Japan had decided to attack Pearl Harbor in order to destroy the US naval fleet in the Pacific Ocean so that Japan could invade and dominate countries in the Pacific without worrying about America's large naval force trying to stop it. But although the attack was successful, it wasn't complete. Eight battleships were sunk or damaged, as were many other ships, and almost two hundred American airplanes. But fortunately for the US Navy, several aircraft carriers were not at Pearl and were not hit, so they could strike back at Japan in the coming months.

President Franklin Delano Roosevelt called December 7, 1941, a "date which will live in infamy." The United States immediately declared war on Japan and, soon after, on Japan's ally Germany. Many Americans didn't want to fight the war before Pearl Harbor, but after the sneak attack, almost everybody was so angry that minds changed overnight.

This turned out to be a mistake, because the Japanese, led by General Tomoyuki Yamashita, the "Tiger of Malaya," swept through the British defenses in a matter of weeks. By February, they had conquered Siam and Malaya and were entering Singapore itself. Frank and the air force he served with were ineffective, and the Japanese established total air superiority over Singapore. They sank the majority of Britain's large naval ships in the Pacific and relentlessly pummeled the troops on the ground.

Fewer than two weeks later, the British were forced—incredibly—to surrender. Singapore was in shock at how fast it had all happened. Many civilians and military personnel were evacuated aboard the few ships that had yet to be sunk by the Japanese, one of which was Judy's *Grasshopper*. The ship was at anchor in Singapore's Keppel Harbor. Frank was among the lucky few allowed to leave. Most servicemen were left behind and were taken captive by the Japanese.

As Japan's army advanced, Keppel Harbor was crowded with refugees of all types. There were retreating soldiers, stoic government workers, terrified Chinese, and stunned colonial families. Some staggered along with everything they owned; others took nothing save the clothing they wore.

All had their eyes on the prize—a place aboard one

Singapore was supposed to be invincible, but the Japanese captured the city shortly after invading. In the final days of British rule, the oil fields near Keppel Harbor were set ablaze to keep them from the Japanese.

© IWM (FE 584)

of the ragtag group of ships that swung at anchor in the harbor, waiting to take them away from the invading Japanese. Wave after wave of refugees crushed toward the makeshift fleet of rescue vessels.

It was February 12, 1942.

Judy watched the chaos below from the deck of the *Grasshopper.* If the mayhem made her particularly nervous, she didn't show it. She sat quietly near the rail, occasionally walking to the other end of the ship, only to return, as if transfixed by the display on the pier.

Judy's nose was incredibly powerful. She had a much better sense of smell than the people all around her. And that was tough, because the harbor stank. The usual waterfront stench of rotting vegetation, fish, and fuel was mixed with the reek of raw sewage—and the overpowering stink of the bombed-out city. The horrible smells of scorched rubber, wood burnt to ash, and the victims of the Japanese invasion made people retch.

Meanwhile, the bombs continued to fall, many right there on the docks. Long stretches of inaction, as the Royal Navy attempted an orderly boarding and escape, were interrupted by dizzying moments of horror as Japanese bombers nicknamed Nells appeared out of nowhere. The shriek of a bomb's approach would join with the cries of those trying to escape it. And then an explosion, often quieter or less dramatic than many expected. Many bombs missed badly, landing in the harbor, sending up fountains of dark water, or, in the city, smashing the homes the people in the harbor had just left, causing flames to leap into the darkening sky. But some bombs struck the dock area, and Judy's floppy ears heard the sounds of people screaming and moaning.

But Judy was a veteran war dog by now, thanks to her service in China. She had seen plenty of suffering and shots fired in anger there. So she remained calm, occasionally running under the steel cover of the bridge when the noise of falling bombs cut through the air. Her ability to sense danger was keeping her alive, but for how much longer?

FLIGHT

The next day, around midmorning, the gunboats were ordered to take on passengers and be ready to leave that evening. Judy was excited, hopping about as the first of the refugees piled onto the *Grasshopper*.

For these unfortunate people, all had been well merely nine weeks before. They were living peaceful lives, filled with family, friends, careers, education, and fun. With sickening speed, all of it had been wrenched away by the invading Japanese. Hopes and dreams were gone, along with many of their possessions and their sense of home. Now survival was all that mattered.

One of Judy's best human friends on the *Grasshopper*

was George White (coincidentally, he came from Frank's hometown, Portsmouth). George was in charge of the ship's food and water supplies, and he had to scramble to find a way to feed the new mouths on board, managing to come up with a cup of tea and a slab of chocolate for every passenger.

Meanwhile, Judy was doing her best to settle the civilians. She was seen constantly nuzzling up to the many crying, frightened children, hoping to give them a familiar and friendly sight, and "personally greeted virtually everyone on board," according to George.

Nearby was another gunboat from the Yangtze River, the *Dragonfly*, along with numerous smaller ships. Two of these were SS *Tien Kwang* and HMS *Kuala*, tanker steamers that were now part of the Royal Navy. Frank and his fellow RAF radarmen were on their way to escape aboard the *Tien Kwang*.

It hadn't exactly been a glorious war thus far for Frank Williams. His radar systems worked badly, if at all, and his air force had been chased from the sky by the Japanese. Now he was retreating madly from an army he and his countrymen had considered harmless mere weeks before.

Upon their arrival at the pier, the RAF evacuees were pointed toward the *Tien Kwang*, and Frank waited in a long line while he and the other 265 radarmen prepared to board, along with numerous army personnel and a handful of civilians. Next door to *Tien Kwang*, the other converted steamer, *Kuala*, had been loaded to bursting, stuffed with refugees and whatever belongings they could squeeze on board; in all, it sailed with between five and six hundred people.

Judy's boat, the *Grasshopper*, captained by Commander Jack Hoffman, pulled away from the docks for good. Screams from the unfortunate civilians left behind trailed the boat as it powered into the harbor.

The *Dragonfly* followed. Out ahead of the gunboats, *Tien Kwang* and *Kuala* were tacking a different course in the same direction. They were all headed for the same place, the city of Batavia, the capital of the Dutch East Indies (the city and the country have since been renamed Jakarta and Indonesia). A large Western presence there promised immediate safety and the likelihood of larger ships for escape to India, Ceylon, or Australia.

But to get to Batavia, they needed to sail across long stretches of ocean, where the Japanese were waiting for them.

ATTACK

The wind howled through Judy's ears as the gunboats pushed hard under the comforting cloak of darkness. The pointer should have been deeply asleep, but noise and people and fear kept her from anything but brief snoozing. She curled up near George on occasion, but just as often lent her comforting presence to the many scared civilians on board. The ship was packed from stem to stern with refugees, most dirty and disheveled, all exhausted by their ordeal. They slept anywhere they could find an unclaimed spot. Judy's warm fur and cold nose were something familiar and happy for them; nothing else was.

Finally, the sun rose, and with it the dread aboard

the gunboats. As the new day, February 14, 1942, began, Japanese flight operations were beginning, and scout planes were taking to the sky. Bomber crews were break-fasting, likely confident of the damage they would inflict that day. Everyone on the *Grasshopper* (except Judy) knew this could well be their last day on earth. The strong among them buried the thought and carried on. For about two hours, the gunboats made good progress, but a few minutes past 9 a.m., their luck ran out.

After her fitful night, Judy had been quiet as day broke, content to make her way around the deck and lie panting in the heat. But now she began a sharp barking. The crew knew what that meant and looked up to the skies. Sure enough, a Japanese seaplane appeared above.

It immediately commenced a dive attack, dropping one bomb at the *Grasshopper* that missed badly, then turn-ing and tossing another bomb at *Dragonfly*. This one was a much better attempt, exploding close enough to the gun-boat to cause slight, but not critical, damage to its bow. The seaplane disappeared, but that was small comfort to those on board the gunboats—the seaplane's big brothers now knew where they were, and a mission was being planned as the damage was assessed.

By eleven thirty, land had been spotted, and the gun-boats closed to within two miles of the island of Posic, a

27

tiny extension of lava and sand that scarcely poked out of the water. Bombers soon appeared in formation out of the south. "Aircraft off the port beam!" someone shouted. Judy was barking madly at them, and the antiaircraft guns opened up.

But there were far too many planes (one *Dragonfly* sailor counted 123) coming in far too fast for any possible defense. Having passed over the ships, they broke formation and attacked in the standard nine-plane groups that had become all too familiar to the sailors and civilians alike.

The bombers, nicknamed Sallies, began their attack runs from between two and four thousand feet above the water and came in five-minute intervals. The ships zigzagged madly in the direction of Posic, hoping to round the island and find some sort of cover. Wave after wave of bombers shrieked overhead, drowning out the screams of the civilians and Judy's angry yelps.

Grasshopper avoided bomb after bomb, but *Dragonfly* wasn't so lucky. It took a direct hit amidships, a blow that practically split the boat in half. Two other bombs connected near the front of the ship (called the bow), including an explosion that laced the bridge area with shrapnel and debris.

Officially, forty crewmen were reported killed, including Malayan crew, in the explosions that ripped the *Dragonfly* apart. Plenty of others remained alive, but desperate. There wasn't much time, as *Dragonfly* was going under fast. It was burning badly in the bow and was splintering down the middle. Several sailors launched a lifeboat and a couple of circular flotation devices called Carley floats.

The *Dragonfly* flopped over on its back, or "turned turtle," as one survivor would say, and sank. "She slid below the sea," wrote Taff Long, a sailor who had managed to jump overboard, "carrying with her the bulk of the ship's company and nearly all the odds and bods we had picked up in Singapore. This all happened in about ten minutes."

The water was thick with thrashing men, making an inviting target for the Sallies, which twice returned to shoot the waterborne men with their machine guns. Long saw them coming and dove as deep as he could to avoid the fire. "As God as my witness—I could hear the bullets hitting the water with a 'zip zip zip,' and I could see the bubbles rising as they penetrated beneath. If I ever prayed I prayed then."

While *Dragonfly* went under, *Grasshopper* was busy trying to avoid the same fate.

It had evaded dozens of bombs, and in so doing had steamed well away from *Dragonfly*, which had run for its life in the opposite direction. The key to the evasive action was a man named Ian Forbes, who had survived being sunk twice in the war already. He now served as a sort of guide dog. "Commander Hoffman was unable to see the aircraft owing to his defective eyesight," Forbes remembered, "so I told him when the bombers were at the point of bomb release and which direction to con [steer] the ship to lay her at right angles to the stick of bombs." But the Sallies kept coming and coming. For nearly two hours, bombs exploded alongside the plucky gunboat, enveloping the ship in geysers of water. Time after time, the *Grasshopper* would pop up from the water with its antiaircraft guns blazing away.

"We avoided between fifteen and twenty attacks," reported Forbes, but at last the falling explosives found the *Grasshopper*, the greenish blue plumes of water replaced with a bright orange tongue of fire. Half a mile out from Posic, a bomb smashed into the mess deck on the aft, or rear, side of the boat. As it happened, this was where a great number of civilians had taken refuge. By sheer ill fortune, after numerous misses, the bomb that finally struck hit home in a most sensitive spot.

Several dozen people were killed outright in the blast. Judy had been with these folks most of the night and had been seen heading belowdecks when the bombing attack began in earnest.

Fire spread through the ship. Hoffman, the skipper, ordered the lifeboats lowered, then stayed on the bridge and rammed the gunboat as close to the shore as he could. The *Grasshopper* couldn't quite make it all the way to the beach. It caught and held on a sandbar about one hundred yards offshore. Hoffman gave the order to abandon ship, and the officers began screaming at everyone left on board to head over the side and into the waist-deep water.

Beached, the *Grasshopper* sat at a shallow angle in the water, low enough that much of the fire was extinguished by the sea, so the danger of explosion was lessened. But the Japanese Sallies hadn't given up. Twice more, the bombs fell, but again missed. Both the gunboat and the passengers who had leapt overboard remained unscathed. This included some Japanese prisoners who were on board. Those prisoners "acted magnificently," in Forbes's words. "All pretense at guarding them was dropped, and they went around calmly and efficiently helping the wounded."

At last, the Sallies disappeared into the clouds. The survivors popped their heads up and looked around. Everyone was happy to be alive, but they were hardly out of danger. They were marooned on a tiny island, with no food or water. Several people were wounded, and there were two hugely pregnant women among the survivors. There was also a blind civilian, tended to at all times by her daughter.

These people had made it through the bombing, but staying alive and getting rescued were hardly things to be counted on at the moment.

Amid all the mayhem, no one noticed that Judy wasn't on the beach.

FRANK'S ESCAPE

Meanwhile, sailing well to the north of Judy was Frank Williams, for whom sleep also came only in fits and starts. He crouched against the railing near the front of the converted steamship *Tien Kwang*, surrounded by more than 250 of his fellow evacuating RAF radarmen.

Passage through the warm and moonless night was mostly uneventful. At dawn, they were within sight of a small island that looked as if it would make a good hiding spot.

It was a tiny piece of coral named Pompong—indeed, calling it an island was generous. The *Tien Kwang* and the *Kuala* anchored in a small, horseshoe-shaped bay at

5:45 a.m. On the *Tien Kwang*, several men volunteered to take the lifeboats and go ashore to collect tree branches, vines, and shrubbery to camouflage the ships, a duty one radarman deemed "a useless operation. It would have taken a week to cut enough branches to cover the two ships."

Unfortunately, the Japanese soon found these two ships as well.

Seventeen planes appeared overhead and began bombing away. *Kuala* took the brunt of the initial damage, with direct hits on the upper bridge, the stokehold (where the boilers were fed with coal), and the engine room. The ship exploded into flames, the fire enveloping the boat. Many were killed instantly. Others jumped over the side of the burning ship. The water was alive with splashing, frantic bodies.

The Japanese noticed the struggle and turned to deliver bombs right on top of the men who were swimming for their lives. What had been an idyllic ocean setting was turned into a slaughterhouse, with dead bodies strewn everywhere.

Even those who reached the shore found it was not necessarily sanctuary. A British nurse named Molly Watts-Carter managed to clamber past the rocks and onto land, finding a cluster of fellow survivors there. "With a small group of seven men I was making a steep hill climb from the beach when the [Japanese] returned. . . . One bomb fell very close to us, killing all my companions and miraculously missing me. I was however numbed by the blast for about fifteen minutes and could not move."

Meanwhile, the bombers turned their attention to *Tien Kwang*, the smaller of the two vessels. A scream went up: "Abandon ship!" Swiftly afterward, a follow-up order: "Take your shoes off before you go in!"

Everyone aboard dove into the water, seemingly all at once. But first, many tossed over the side anything that could possibly float; a man named Wang Hua-Nan grabbed an armchair and heaved it into the salt water, hoping it would help get him the short distance to shore, as he could not swim.

They had just started swimming for Pompong when the first bombs fell. None hit the ship—they exploded in the water atop the men instead.

Other aircraft added machine-gun fire to the storm of steel. The planes shot at the desperate swimmers with bullets. Many were killed. No one can be sure exactly how many.

Frank recalled the moment years later by noting, "The lifeboats were destroyed and we were forced to jump into the water. We had to swim about three hundred meters [nearly a thousand feet] to reach the shore, hoping that the exploding bombs scattered the nearby sharks. The water between the ship and the shore was filled with drowning men when the second wave arrived for the deathblow. The squadron...made a reconnaissance flight of the battered ship, turned in a wide arc and released their remaining bombs over the drowning men at mast height. Dozens died in this cowardly attack."

But Frank wasn't one of them. It appears Frank was closer to the island than many of his fellow swimmers, either because he was stronger in the water or because his seamanship, honed by his time in the merchant navy, allowed him to get overboard more quickly and to get into better position than the others. It might well have been mere good luck. Whatever the cause, he escaped the worst of the bombs and was able to stagger onto Pompong in one piece.

One man refused the order to go over the side; he was an electrician and engineer for the Malayan government named Charles Baker. Baker had evacuated aboard the *Kuala* but rowed over at first light to the *Tien Kwang* when asked to have a look at a conked-out engine that was puzzling its crew. The attack commenced just after he went belowdecks. Baker stayed and made the fixes, amazed that no bombs actually hit the boat.

He had made his way back topside when someone

yelled to him, "Look at your bloody ship!" *Kuala* was burning furiously, on the verge of destruction. Baker dove into the ocean as another wave of bombers swooped in. Giant waterspouts erupted as the explosions went off. Miraculously unhurt, Baker made for the burning *Kuala*, but the fire was far too strong. So Baker turned toward Pompong. He was headed for a clump of women struggling in the water when a burst from a falling bomb rattled him, causing his false teeth to fly out and "sink forever."

Toothless, he pulled three women to shore by their life belts.

Moments later, the *Kuala* slipped away. The bombs that hit its engine room had destroyed the steam pipes required for firefighting, so there was little anyone could do to save *Kuala*.

For whatever reason, the ocean currents were stronger by the *Tien Kwang* than they were a few hundred yards away, where the *Kuala* survivors weren't badly affected. Wang Hua-Nan and his armchair missed landfall and drifted past "numerous floating bodies, both living and dead" out to sea. His armchair soon broke apart. "I succeeded in getting hold of two... corpses, both of which had life jackets on and were within my reach," he later wrote in a letter to a friend. Wang used a money belt he wore to tie himself to the dead bodies, then floated for

37

hours, somehow surviving in waters "infested with sharks and crocodiles."

Another raft carrying thirty civilians from the *Kuala* was swept past Pompong and out into open waters, but mostly, it was the radarmen off the *Tien Kwang* who were unable to reach shore. Some would drift for days, eventually washing up on other islands or getting picked up by fishing skiffs. Far more perished in a watery death. Frank was extremely lucky. Of the 266 radarmen aboard, 179 were killed in the attack. Only thirty-four of them would eventually reach safety in Ceylon. The other fifty-three, Frank included, would suffer a different fate.

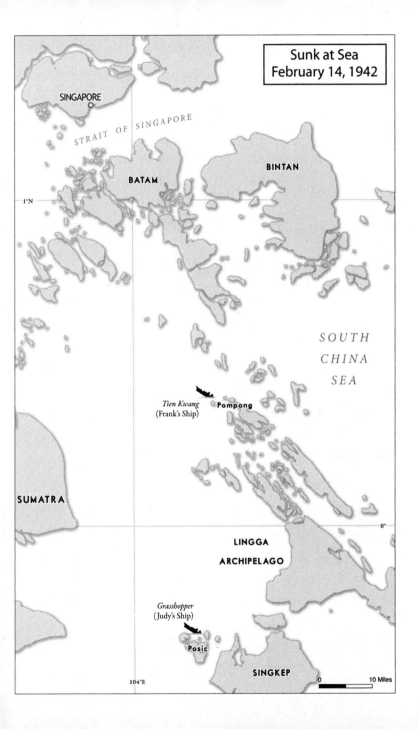

Sunk at Sea
February 14, 1942

SINGAPORE

STRAIT OF SINGAPORE

BATAM

BINTAN

1°N

SOUTH
CHINA
SEA

Tien Kwang
(Frank's Ship)   **Pompong**

SUMATRA

0°

LINGGA

ARCHIPELAGO

Grasshopper
(Judy's Ship)   **Posic**

SINGKEP

104°E   0   10 Miles

SAVING JUDY

The *Grasshopper* and *Dragonfly* survivors gathered on the sandy beach of Posic, the tiny island where they had washed ashore. The beach was small, quickly giving way to a dense jungle "thick with closely packed trees from which hung a tangled mess of thorns," one survivor wrote. "However careful one was, it was impossible not to get scratched." Posic appeared to be uninhabited, but Hoffman ordered a small motorboat that had survived the attack to circumnavigate the island just to make sure. He then barked at Forbes, who had just survived his third sinking of the war, to "Go and get help!" Forbes grabbed two others and set off on foot.

After a few hours, it was apparent that there was not

only no one living on Posic but also no fresh water on the island. This meant the survivors faced few options, none of them good. They could wait on the sand until they were captured or died of thirst, or they could cram as many women as possible into the small whaler and have the men swim for it, hoping to survive the sharks and the current until they found another island—one that hopefully had water. Neither option held much appeal.

Australian War Memorial

The Japanese destroyed almost every ship fleeing Singapore in mid-February 1942. Lifeboats dotted the South China Sea in the aftermath of the destruction.

George hoped there was still some food or water on the *Grasshopper*. Hoffman asked George if he would go check out the ship once the motorboat returned from its exploration. George shook his head at the delay and volunteered to swim over to the ship at once. Time was of the essence. He immediately regretted his decision as he walked toward the surf. A dead shark, longer than George by about three feet, lay on the beach. It wasn't clear if the monster fish had been killed by exploding bombs or taken down by an even larger shark, but whatever the cause of death, George was shaken by the sight. Ever stalwart, he peeled off his shirt and dove into the warm water.

Setting his personal best in the freestyle, George covered the hundred yards or so to the smoldering *Grasshopper*. He made his way below, pushing into the officers' quarters. He recovered several things of value, including pots, pans, and cutlery. But no food or water.

He then made his way to the forecastle deck, where the ship's lockers were. In the near darkness, as he slogged through the water, George's mind began to drift into the unknown, and he suddenly felt quite afraid. Then he heard an inhuman whine, almost a moaning. Goose bumps erupted on his skin. "I've never been that scared, even when the bombs were falling," he later said. But despite the frightening sound, duty called. He had to push through to

42

the last portion of the locker area to complete his search. Gathering all his courage, he was entering the room at the end of the partially submerged hall when the moan was heard again.

This time, however, George's fear was replaced by elation, for he recognized the noise—it was Judy!

In the chaos and hubbub of the bombing, sinking, and rush for survival, no one had taken note of the ship's canine crew member, not even George himself. During the attack, Judy had instinctively gone below to take cover. She had been in this room, which was near her usual sleeping berth, when a bomb sent several of the ship's lockers crashing against the wall. They didn't fall entirely to the floor, which would have crushed the dog. Instead, they trapped her in a small pocket against the bulkhead, where she could more or less stand in the water, using the sunken gunboat's angle to her advantage. But she couldn't escape. George followed the noise to the fallen lockers and ran his hands behind them. He felt wet, matted fur, then a dry ear, and then a cold nose. Judy licked the hands, not knowing or caring who they belonged to.

George managed to pin himself against the lockers, and using his weight as a lever, he moved them enough for Judy to escape the trap and splash into the open area beyond. George carried her up the ladder to the deck. He suspected the poor dog was hurt, scared, and exhausted. The ordeal of the sinking had nearly done him in, he reckoned. What chance did a dog have?

To his amazement, after a moment, Judy stood up, furiously shook herself dry, and ran over to him, eagerly licking his face, ready to play. To the sailor, Judy's relief was palpable. George recalled that he didn't know whether to laugh or cry.

"Why didn't you bark?" he asked Judy. "I'd have come for you a lot sooner."

Then man and dog returned to the deck of the *Grasshopper*, where George yelled the first good news of the day to the survivors.

"Hey, I found Judy! She's alive!"

A cheer rang out from the beach.

George constructed a makeshift raft from loose timber and piled the few treasures he could salvage aboard it. He was on his knees, trying to steer the unwieldy craft with Judy standing next to him. It was awkward, and George was doing his best to manage the current when Judy suddenly barked loudly and jumped into the water.

She swam strongly in circles around the raft. George was puzzled by her behavior until he saw a dark shadow pass under him, sweeping the seafloor. His first thought was that a Japanese submarine had somehow found them.

Then he realized he was watching a large shark, most likely a deadly tiger shark, cruise by.

Judy kept barking. She would have been a tasty snack for the mammoth shark, but it wasn't hungry or the ruckus scared it off. Either way, George sped for the nearby beach and soon ran aground, with Judy bounding from the surf just ahead of him.

"I was quite sure Judy had sensed the danger and did what she could to protect me," George later wrote. "She was clearly at the shark's mercy, but true to her nature, she dove right in regardless." The incident was similar to one back in China, when Judy had warned a sailor named Charles Jeffery away from a prowling leopard.

Amazingly, Judy's heroics had only just begun.

POSIC ISLAND

Having looked out for George's life in the surf, Judy now turned to the rest of the survivors. She began sprinting up and down the beach, actively sniffing the sand, at times plunging into the water, which was receding at low tide. After a while, one of the survivors looked up from the fire he was building to yell to George.

"Hey, Chief, I think your dog has found a bone or something."

George went over to where Judy was furiously digging at the sand. Expecting her to have found something that appealed only to dogs, he was shocked when a burble of water popped up from the wet sand.

"Water!" he yelled. "Judy's found us fresh water!"

George went to help. He started digging, too. Soon a geyser of lifesaving water erupted from the sand. George and several men caught as much as they could in the pots he had rescued from the *Grasshopper*, and the haul was rationed among the group. There was enough to make cocoa and rice for dinner. One of the party lifted his cocoa. "To Judy," he toasted. Judy looked around at the mention of her name, wagged her tail, and went back to snoozing, snuggled neatly between a pair of survivors.

A little later, a group of survivors from the *Dragonfly* made it to Posic. One of them was a man named Les Searle who had gotten to know Judy back in Singapore. Despite the peril he was in, Les was overjoyed to see the pointer still alive and sniffing.

The first night was spent shivering. No one could believe how cold it was. These were the tropics, after all. But when the sun went down, teeth started to chatter. The sole light came from the still-burning *Grasshopper*, and the blaze only got stronger as the hour grew later. A survivor named J. A. C. Robins described how the fire "had now got a firm hold and was burning fiercely, the flames making a lurid glow through the trees. Small arms ammo was going off continuously; occasionally shells would burst and seemed to whistle away into the distance. We felt uncomfortably close to her. After an hour or two of this there was a terrific explosion as the magazine blew up, the air was filled with sparks like a gigantic fireworks display and a shower of burning material came down on the trees around us."

If George hadn't gone aboard and discovered Judy, she would have perished in the blast.

Another man joined the group the second day—Taff Long, the sailor from the *Dragonfly* who had dodged the bullets in the water. He stumbled into the mob of ragged survivors on the beach. "What a shambles!" he recorded.

> *Wounded people were lying everywhere. There was no medical supplies—there was no food and precious little water. What water they had had been found by Judy, the pointer that had been the* Grasshopper's *mascot.... There were half-a-dozen dead who had been laid some distance away as there were no tools to bury them...I found myself a space in the sand and settled down for the night.*

At this point Forbes, probably feeling invincible, decided to push his already remarkable luck. He was granted permission to swim to an island nearby, one he had seen during the attack, to seek help.

Again, night fell on Posic. The only light came from the stars, which shone brilliantly over the ocean, seemingly close enough to touch. Judy did her part to sustain spirits. Then the daughter of the blind woman came to George with troubling news—the two pregnant women were about to give birth.

As it happened, there was an experienced midwife among them. George had helped deliver a baby on board a navy ship during the Spanish Civil War, and he felt comfortable doing it again. There were nurses on Posic, but they couldn't be spared, so off he went, with only the young girl as an assistant. Fortunately, all went well. Two boys were delivered safely and were baptized in the sea the next day. The grateful mothers named their newborns George and Leonard (White's middle name) in his honor.

For four more days, the survivors clung to life, living on coconuts and water. "The wounded were pitiful to see and suffered greatly," according to Taff. The beach camp was virtually overrun by ants, tiny sand lice, and biting fleas. The insects made life miserable for the group, who were also plagued by spiders and lizards that went directly for the dwindling food supply. But worst was the ever-present threat of poisonous snakes. Several species of dangerous reptiles teemed across the atoll, including coral snakes, banded kraits, and several varieties of cobras and pit vipers.

Judy stood guard against the snakes. She would leap up and engage an unseen threat in the sand or at the nearby tree line. She would buck about like a bronco, using her exceptional quickness to stay away from the flashing fangs. Generally, the reptile, hissing and angry, would back off, but if it didn't, Judy would strike with her paw or teeth until the snake was dead. She would then scoop it up and deposit it at the feet of a horrified human survivor. After a while, though, the people realized that the snakes sometimes made for a decent dinner.

Judy was doing her part, but if rescue didn't come soon, the group would either starve or be forced to sail the whaler into the unknown, a few people at a time.

Then, salvation. At last, as night fell on the fifth day after the *Grasshopper* was sunk, a shout went up. "Boat!" A large local fishing boat known as a tongkang was headed to shore, a rescue ship sent by the incredible Ian Forbes. Under cover of darkness, the remaining survivors were ferried off Posic in waves, headed for a larger island nearby.

Thanks to guts, blind luck, and the superhuman nose of a dog named Judy, they had survived being cast away on a desert island. But their troubles were only beginning. Safety was still a long way off, and the Japanese could undo their efforts at any moment.

Numerous survivors were plucked from remote islands and brought to (temporary) safety. This vessel, SS Krait, piloted by an Australian named Bill Reynolds, ferried an estimated two thousand people in the waters off Sumatra during the chaos.

POMPONG

Things were bad for Frank Williams, too. Like Judy, he was stranded on an uninhabited island with scores of wounded, many of them civilians. Rescue would be problematic, given the number of castaways and the prowling Japanese airplanes and ships, hungry for more targets.

Frank assisted in the first order of business, which was to carry the wounded to a clearing in the jungle about one hundred feet above sea level. One female survivor later described the area in the following way: "In normal times it would have been an ideal picnic site; now it resembled a small battlefield." Pompong Island was about half a mile long and three-quarters of a mile wide, with a spiny backbone of rock running down the middle that loomed roughly four hundred feet over the water. The land rose steeply out of the ocean, and rocks made getting in and out of the sea difficult.

Just over six hundred people had made it to safety in two main groups, and they now collected to form a huge party. Everyone was in need of food and water. Some tins of bully beef (also known as corned beef) had been rescued from the *Tien Kwang* before it sank, but there was no fresh water. Luckily, a search party discovered a small spring. It "slowly but regularly dripped drinkable water," Frank remembered.

Wing Commander Farwell, RAF, took charge of the military men, and Reginald Nunn, the head of the public works department in Singapore, was elected to command the civilian government workers. The *Kuala*'s chief engineer built a canopy of branches and vines to give the wounded some relief from the blazing sun.

But even among the death and destruction, there was a glimmer of hope, just as there had been on Posic: a new life. A baby was born to a pregnant woman named Mrs. Jones.

Frank spent a good deal of his first day on the island working with other parties on the unenviable task of moving the many corpses that washed up on the beach. There wasn't much deep soil to work with, and the men often had to go well into the jungle to find proper resting places, generally leaving the bodies in heavy bush when they couldn't dig holes.

The RAF men separated into their own group near the spring. Just walking around was tough, as most had lost their shoes in the attack. There wasn't much to do except watch the clouds pass across the sky and count the minutes until chow time, which would soften the rumbling in their stomachs. But little could distract them from the painful cries of the wounded and the realization that they were in deep trouble.

Rations were enforced, and each survivor was given two cups of water per day. The bully beef was plentiful, but it wasn't known how long it would be needed. So twelve people would split a tin apiece twice a day. They also were given some condensed milk and two biscuits per day.

The first night passed uneventfully, though the bitter cold caught the lightly dressed survivors off guard and added to the overall misery. Campfires were ruled out, as they had been on Posic, for fear of attracting enemy aircraft. The people slept clasped tightly to one another for warmth.

The next day was Sunday, February 15, and plenty of prayer was heard around Pompong that morning. As if in response, a British sailor soon puttered up in a local tong-kang. He was the first rescuer to arrive at Pompong. First the badly wounded were evacuated. Then hundreds of women and children were taken off the island by a large vessel. Tragically, it was torpedoed by the Japanese, and most aboard were killed.

The remaining men (and one lone woman, Gertrude Nunn, Reginald's wife, who insisted on staying behind) knew nothing of this bitter turn of fate. By Tuesday the seventeenth, the lack of food was beginning to wear on the survivors who remained on Pompong, even though there were far fewer of them to feed. The men lay around, hungry and listless. "Any exertion needed considerable willpower," according to one man left on the island. John Williams (no relation to Frank) remembered, "We seemed condemned to one of two fates, either to die of starvation or to be found by the [Japanese] and summarily disposed of, as were other parties in similar circumstances. We were fairly weak and mostly lay down whilst a few kept lookout in the rather forlorn hope that another friendly ship might come to our help."

At last, on February 20, as Frank and the other servicemen left on Pompong could think of nothing except their own hunger and despair, they were rescued. Another British man was sailing around the area, having heard there were still some people in bad shape on the tiny islands. Frank and his buddies were smashed like sardines into the hold of the man's forty-foot boat, but at least they were on the move once again.

"How we managed to maneuver that vessel remains a mystery to me," Frank remembered of the tongkang, hardly anyone's first choice for a desperate voyage on the open ocean. Then there was the continuing threat from airplanes with the blood red sun of the Japanese flag painted on them. "Two times Japanese airplanes passed over us, but they let us be," Frank said. Soon enough, he arrived at Dabo, the main port city of Singkep, the large island that anchored the group that included Pompong and Posic. Judy had just arrived there, too.

Both were safe—for the moment, anyway.

JUNGLE TREK

Neither Frank nor Judy stayed very long on Singkep. Like everyone who had raced out of Singapore the week before and had been attacked in the ocean by the Japanese, they had a new destination to shoot for.

Due west was the massive island of Sumatra, the largest in the Dutch East Indies. On the far western side was a port city called Padang. There, ships were waiting to take as many survivors as possible to India, where the Japanese were not. This meant the survivors had to go back out on the ocean to get to Sumatra, then cut across the interior to get to Padang and, hopefully, safety.

Before leaving, Judy said good-bye to a close companion.

George decided, in what he later called "something of a lunatic choice," to split off from the group making its way to Sumatra. Instead, he and a handful of others opted to sail directly for India.

"I was firmly convinced that there was no longer safety in numbers and that the Japanese would eventually round up all refugees and escapees," George recalled later. "I also decided I was not going to be around when they did so. Judy seemed to understand all that was going on and licked my hand before I turned away." Incredibly, George would survive the long voyage in a very small boat. Using nothing but a page ripped from a schoolboy atlas for navigation, and despite sickness, hunger, and the constant threat of discovery, George landed with three other men in India. It was an amazing feat.

Meanwhile, Judy went looking for a new friend. Frank was right there on the island, but the dog chose a more familiar face. She found Les Searle and made him and his group of pals her new favorites. Les's clique also included a large Scotsman named John "Jock" Devani, an accomplished scrounger and "the bravest man I've ever known," according to Les. Judy curled up alongside these sailors for much of the boat trip to Sumatra, her nose between her paws. Even Judy needed some sleep once in a while.

The pointer and her friends found their way to Sumatra,

then continued up a river to a town called Rengat. But they arrived to find that there were no cars or trucks or anything with wheels to transport them farther west to Padang. "The escape organization was closing down by the time we arrived," Taff Long reported. "It was every man for himself."

Judy's group met up with a few locals who gave them some food. The poor dog needed every crumb. The locals also showed them the river path that would take them across Sumatra—on foot, roughly 170 miles through some of the thickest, creepiest jungle on the planet.

Judy and a group of around fifteen navy men, including Les, Jock, and Taff, were feeling desperate to move on. The Japanese could be there any minute. To be captured now, after surviving the bombing and the desert island, was terrifying. Because of that fear, men and dog took the risk and disappeared into the jungle.

It was a horrible place, wet and dangerous. Various vipers, cobras, and kraits slithered under logs and rocks, while in the trees, the largest snake in the world, the reticulated python, waited to snatch prey and kill with its bone-crushing squeeze. Among the arachnids in the jungle, the scorpion-tailed spider was particularly ghoulish, with its long, spiky appendage trailing off its standard eight-legged body.

The enormous wilderness contained mammals from colossal elephants to dangerous tapirs and rhinos, from the beautiful clouded leopard and its fierce relative the black leopard to the world's only venomous primate, the slow loris (which is actually quite quick when scared).

The most dangerous were the Sumatran tigers, which are now almost extinct but at that time still stalked the forest interior.

And, of course, there were crocodiles, lots and lots of crocodiles. Of all the natural threats in the jungle, they posed the greatest threat to man and dog.

The plant life the group encountered was likewise outsized, unique, and dangerous. A huge portion of the Sumatran rain forest today is gone, its lumber taken in the name of profit, a practice called "clear-cutting." During the time Judy picked her way through the trees, this hadn't yet begun in earnest, leaving the wild growth unspoiled. Beautiful rare orchids grew under towering bamboo trees anchored by enormous roots. In the undergrowth, carnivorous plants called monkey cups snacked on unlucky insects.

The group found the river soon enough, as it ran only a few hundred yards from the outskirts of the village. Already, any signs of civilization had been wiped from view by the trees and vines and darkness. As soon as they turned west, Judy took point position and ranged ahead of the party, on the lookout for any potential danger. She was easy to spot, as someone had slipped a navy cap onto her head just before they set off.

"What a sight we must have been leaving Rengat," remembered Taff. "Some with no shoes—ragged, filthy shorts, some with native clip-clops [thick sandals].... We had no money—no soap—no provisions."

According to Les, Judy felt like the group "belonged to her." The way she acted, he said later, was as though she were single-handedly responsible for the safe transit to Padang. She was tireless in the jungle, loping from front to back of the group, sniffing madly with her powerful nose. She was on the alert. Her long ears pricked up at the slightest noise rumbling out of the darkness.

Soon they were in the heart of the jungle. Walking was extremely difficult. The heat was amplified by the intense humidity. The survivors' clothes were soaked with sweat within minutes and wouldn't dry for the entire journey. Huge roots and overgrown branches blocked their path. Thick, sucking mud was everywhere. The gooey muck was full of leeches, which attached themselves to exposed skin and could only be detached by flame. If a leech was pulled off once it attached itself, there was not only pain but also an open wound to contend with. In that climate, the wound would fester into a tropical ulcer in no time. Jock, the Scotsman, found a leech on his groin early in the march. He had to grit his teeth and singe the leech off, managing not to permanently injure himself in the process.

Judy's nose and ears were crucial to the group's safety, but so were her paws. With all the deep mud around, the dog spent plenty of time finding solid ground on which to walk. As the party's ranger, she took it upon herself to find the best pathway, and her barks signaled the group to follow her lead—indeed, to stay in her footsteps where, at times, the land was as narrow as Judy herself.

On the second day of the trek, the survivors had their first brush with the dangers of the jungle. A short time after breakfast, Judy was running ahead as usual when she stopped short and growled loudly. Everyone froze. After a moment, a large crocodile sloshed into the water off the path about twenty feet in front of the pointer.

Before anyone could thank Judy for the heads-up, she continued her barking, chasing the croc up the river. She might have been trying to scare off any attack or merely showing a bit of territorial dominance, but whatever the reason, she got a little too close to the enormous reptile, which turned and lunged at her. With a midair twist, Judy managed to miss the slashing jaws by an inch ("I thought for sure she was dead," Les would later recount), but the croc raked her across the shoulder with its claws. She yelped and backpedaled furiously. The crocodile took the opportunity to escape instead of pressing the attack, but it most likely could have bitten Judy in half had it chosen to chase her.

Jock was the first of the party to reach Judy and eyeball the damage. The croc had cut a six-inch slice into the dog, though miraculously it wasn't too deep. There was blood, but it was a small wound that could be patched up with the limited first aid supplies the group possessed. Knowing how important Judy was to the success of their trek, the group stopped to carefully tend to the dog when they reached an abandoned warehouse a couple of hours later. But the animal that had survived a dunking in the Yangtze, a ship being bombed out from under her, and a desert island wasn't about to let a prehistoric beast end her life. Soon enough, they were on their way again, Judy in front as usual.

Despite Judy's brave efforts, it was a painful trek for the men. "We lived either off the land on bananas, pineapples, etc. when we came upon them, or went hungry," wrote Taff. "When we reached a native village we either depended on their generosity for a meager gift of rice or, failing co-operation, took food by other methods. We were desperate men."

Judy wouldn't require much medical attention, but soon the other members of the party began dropping like flies. A twisted ankle here, symptoms of malaria there, exhaustion everywhere. The unit had to stop to make stretchers from trees and roots to carry the afflicted. Utter fatigue settled over them. The single-file trekkers got spread out, forcing Judy to double back to encourage and safely guide the stragglers, using even more energy.

Whenever anyone got tired, Judy was there to bark, wag her tail, lick muddy faces, whatever it took, despite the fact that she herself was caked in muck. She would disappear into the distance ahead and return with (mostly) edible small animals, even winged ones like bats, to add to the food on hand. On several other occasions, she sniffed out crocodiles lying in ambush and barked until they moved on. She had learned her lesson, though, and stayed out of reach.

At one point, deep into the slog, Les heard a ferocious growl unlike any he had heard before. Assuming it was Judy, he whistled for her and set off toward the noise, hoping she wasn't hurt again. Judy appeared, but behind him. She was actually chasing after him and was barking furiously. Wondering what had been the source of the original growl—and not wanting to find out—Les began to back away slowly. There was a flash of brownish orange to his left, and the crashing of brush. Judy kept up her loud barking as Les raced back to the group. While he could never be positive, he was convinced he had just had a close encounter with the rare but deadly Sumatran tiger. He was also certain it had been Judy's barking that prevented the beast from attacking, just as Judy had scared the shark away from George White. Many kinds of man-eating animals had met their match with this dog—only the crocodile stuck around to challenge her.

The refugees wandered on. "We climbed and descended mountains, waded through swamps and small rivers and finally reached the railhead in a sorry state," Taff wrote. At last, after roughly three weeks of trudging through the rain forest, the group straggled into Sawah Luento, a town of about fifteen thousand inhabitants—where a train that would take them the final fifty miles into Padang left every day. "We were overjoyed to be informed that a train could take us... that very afternoon," recalled Taff.

Their goal was within reach, practically close enough for Judy to sniff.

The final stage of the Sumatra crossing—the train between Sawah Luento and Padang, the coastal town that promised freedom.

PADANG

Frank and his friends from Pompong Island were racing toward freedom as well. But unlike Judy and her group, they didn't have to walk.

Frank sailed to Sumatra aboard a locally owned boat, just as Judy had, and then up the same river to Rengat. It was there that he caught a glimpse of his future.

In an amazing detail from an interview Frank gave in 1970, he said it was in Rengat where he first laid eyes on Judy. "I did not know who she was or where she came from," he remembered. "Only later was I told that she was one of the survivors of HMS *Grasshopper*. I remember thinking, 'What on earth is a beautiful English pointer like that doing over here with no one to care for her?'...I realized that even though she looked thin and frail she was a true survivor."

But the Japanese army was advancing relentlessly, so there was no time for Frank to get a proper introduction to his future best friend. The dog disappeared into the jungle shortly afterward.

Unlike Judy's unlucky group, Frank managed to find his way onto a truck leaving the small city, heading west. It was hardly first-class transport. "For the most part they were incredibly ramshackle," noted a British report on the vehicles, "yet they tirelessly made journey after journey carrying full loads." "We arrived in one piece," remembered a British artilleryman named John Purvis. "I don't know how we did it."

Frank and many of the RAF shipwreck survivors piled into trucks for the crossing to Sawah Luento. From there, they boarded the train that left for Padang every afternoon, winding through the mountain passes that guarded the seaside town. Frank was on a train that left Sawah Luento on March 7 or 8, a week before Judy's group hopped on a train in the same direction.

For the first time since leaving Singapore, Frank and his friends could feel a bit optimistic. The group could practically taste the ocean breeze, imagine themselves leaning over the rail of a safe and sturdy ship, and feel a comfortable bed. None of them were cowards; every one of them would have gone back to fight immediately if asked. They just needed a short break. And they were so close to getting one.

Frank's train pulled into the Padang train station with a clatter and the screaming hiss of the brakes. The first thing Frank and the RAF men did was to report to the few British officers left in town. The officer in charge was a Royal Marines colonel named Alan Warren, a tall, ramrod-straight man with a black mustache and an iron will. Warren asked for volunteers to help the Dutch fighters defend the town. Almost everyone, Frank included, submitted their names for service, but the Dutch commander politely turned them down. The Brits didn't have much jungle fighting experience, it was explained. They would need to be equipped with arms and gear that couldn't be spared, and their recent experiences escaping Singapore had left them far from fit. Frank and the other RAF men had to admit that was true.

In the end, it didn't matter. The word had come through the jungle from the Japanese—resistance was futile and would be punished. Should the city be declared "open," it would not be bombed.

The Dutch authorities agreed to those terms. That

meant the city of Padang was spared, but everyone there would become prisoners unless they could be rescued by ship.

Sadly for Frank and Judy, on March 7, just before Frank's train pulled into Padang and while Judy was still pushing through the deep, dark jungle, SS *Pelapo* pulled up its anchor and sped away from the port of Emmahaven with fifty servicemen aboard. *Pelapo* would be the final escape boat out.

Frank's and Judy's last-gasp dash for rescue came up just a bit short.

One ship, a British cruiser, was circling offshore for nearly a week, awaiting the code signal to approach. But the British officials had burned the code books to keep them out of enemy hands. Without the proper codes, the men on land couldn't coordinate a rescue. When Frank and the other RAF men learned there was no way out, they got extremely angry. First the British forces had been chased out of Singapore by the Japanese. Now the military couldn't even radio a rescue ship steaming just over the horizon. Frank was trapped in Padang, frustrated and helpless.

A few men, eighteen to be exact, weren't trapped. Colonel Warren decided they were vital to the war effort, and so they slipped out of Padang disguised as native fishermen (amazingly, they made it all the way to Ceylon, now called Sri Lanka).

War forces commanders to make very difficult choices—often, they must choose who lives and who dies among the men who serve under them. This was a classic example. The colonel selected people to escape the clutches of the Japanese, leaving Frank and his fellow radarmen to be captured. Frank wasn't the kind to complain about it, but he couldn't have been happy with the decision.

There would be no fight to hold the city. Even worse, the Dutch concentrated on preventing anyone from slipping away. Small boats were scattered about, but the Dutch made them off-limits. "To our dismay," Frank recalled, "the civilian harbor authorities refused to transfer ownership of these boats to us out of fear of Japanese retribution. They even disabled them." A handful of men beat the system by volunteering to patrol the harbor to prevent boats from being stolen. Once on the job, these men found a boat they could handle and set out to sea. Another group stole a boat but were ultimately captured by the Dutch and handed over to the Japanese.

So Frank settled in, hoping against hope that he would be rescued, as he had been on Pompong Island. At least Padang was a more pleasant place to be stuck, despite the small earthquake that shook the city while the men waited.

71

The sixty thousand inhabitants of the city enjoyed paved streets and well-stocked shops. As Stanley Saddington of the RAF would recall, Padang had "all the signs of a well-run and peaceful little town." Green mountains up to twelve thousand feet high towered over Padang, adding to the beauty of the landscape, which also had the ocean view to the west. There was also a suburbia of sorts, with villages well away from the city center. The officers were housed in fine hotels, while the rank and file made do with an old gymnasium. The evenings were eerily quiet, thanks to a curfew. Schools had canceled classes, performing arts centers shut down, and government services ground to a halt.

All that was left to do was to wait for the Japanese to arrive and take them prisoner.

Into this setting of hopelessness bounded Judy the pointer.

MEETING THE ENEMY

"There's the sea!" someone yelled when the train carrying Judy and her friends crested a hill to show Padang glistening on the shore of the Indian Ocean. "What a sight!" remembered Taff. "The first ray of hope for nearly a month." After an overnight journey, the train clanked into the station early on the morning of March 16. The engine hadn't even stopped before the members of the group were helping each other off and bombarding anyone they passed with questions about getting out on the next ship.

It was a grizzled old local man who broke their hearts. "The last ship left already—you just missed it." Actually, it had been nine days since the *Pelapo* had disappeared over the horizon, which was not exactly just missing it. But the essence of the old man's statement was spot-on. After all this group had been through, the critical delays had cost them everything.

When the group reported to a startled Colonel Warren, he sympathized with their plight, but he was also blunt: Don't consider fighting—the surrender is already arranged. Don't try to steal local watercraft—you'll be captured and punished. Feel free to return to the jungle (hardly an option after the walkabout they had already taken).

The survivors seemed to collectively lose hope. "Despondency and despair descended on all," recalled Taff. According to Les, Judy seemed to sense the depression that hovered over her friends. Dogs are quite capable of that kind of intuition. That's one of the reasons canines went from wild animal to domestic pet. Humans enjoyed having another creature around that seemed to understand them.

Judy likely would have tried to be extra friendly and attentive during this period, despite her exhaustion, in order to lift the spirits of her human friends. It was behavior totally in character for this particular pointer.

Hoping against hope, the band spent the night at the dock, scanning the sea, desperately trying to wish a friendly boat into existence. But none came. They were ordered to move into a local Dutch school. Frank was down the street in Padang's Chinese school.

It was Judy who first alerted her friends to the arrival of the dreaded enemy. She was in the center of the small classroom she had claimed, resting her head on her forelegs as she did when lying still, staring at the door. When she stood and began to bristle, her lip tensed in a silent snarl, and everyone in the room knew their time was up. Motorcycles were heard, and Judy started to bark. Les tore a piece of cloth from his pants and slipped it through Judy's collar, pulling her closer to him.

A Japanese colonel and his staff soon entered the room with a flourish. The officer had thick glasses and a professorial air, but his sharp, clipped burst of words established his immediate command of the situation. He pointed to Judy and said something in Japanese that no one caught, abruptly turned on his heel, and left. Les and the others with guns were disarmed, and then they were left alone to ponder their fate.

The colonel went to the Chinese school next and took visible glee in smashing a portrait of General Chiang Kai-shek, the leader of the Chinese government and enemy of Japan (see sidebar), to smithereens. He next proceeded to the office of the head Dutch administrator in Padang; Colonel Warren later gave his impressions:

They strode purposefully in with the air of conquerors, kicking their legs in front of them, their muddy boots striking heavily on the floor, their curved swords jangling as they walked....These were good fighting men, crude, fierce, proud and confident. There was little about the undersized, myopic [Japanese officer] in this bunch with the broad flat, yellow faces and long whispy [sic] mustaches.

GENERAL CHIANG KAI-SHEK

When Judy lived in China, the leader of the country was named Chiang Kai-shek. He was the head of a government called the *Kuomintang*, which means Nationalist Party. His title was Generalissimo, which sounds strange but is a fancy way of saying that Chiang was the highest-ranking military officer in the country.

Chiang was friendly with Western countries like the United States and England, but he had enemies. Mainly, the Communist Party of China fought long and hard against Chiang, so there was a civil war going on in China even as they also fought the Japanese.

The Japanese invasion forced Chiang to flee to the Chinese countryside, but he stayed in command of most of the national armed forces. When World War Two broke out in the Pacific, Chiang became an important military leader, often taking part in big discussions of strategy with President Franklin Delano Roosevelt and Winston Churchill, the prime minister of Great Britain.

Chiang was married to a woman named Soong May-Ling, better known as Madame Chiang. She had gone to school in America and was well known for giving speeches across the United States trying to get the US to support China. She was very successful, and many Americans felt a special friendship with China during this period because of her.

All night Judy's group discussed their situation. Everyone had heard the fates of those unfortunate enough to be taken by the Japanese. The Imperial Japanese Army at the time sneered at military types who chose surrender over death, and thus they held little respect for prisoners of war. Japan had never fully agreed to the Geneva Conventions (see sidebar), notifying enemy countries through its Foreign Affairs Ministry that the Conventions would be applied only as they saw fit. The Japanese statement was open-ended and allowed them to do whatever they pleased to those who had been captured. Indeed, many defendants at later war crime tribunals knew nothing of the Conventions and said they had no idea they were committing crimes.

THE GENEVA CONVENTIONS

When soldiers are wounded or taken prisoner during a war, they are protected against any more bad treatment by the enemy. That's thanks to a series of laws called the Geneva Conventions. The word *convention* in this case means not a gathering of a large group of people but an agreement between countries, like a treaty.

Basically, the laws make sure that armies that win won't be overly cruel to the defeated. That is especially true of the Convention that covers prisoners of war (POWs). This agreement was signed in 1929 by fifty-three countries.

Japan signed the Convention, but then ignored it during World War Two. POWs were supposed to be held in healthy camps similar to army bases. They were supposed to be well fed and well treated and given good medical care. Frank and Judy and the other prisoners of the Japanese got none of this. The Japanese believed that dying in battle was glorious. If you were taken prisoner, you were a failure and a coward. So they treated their prisoners without respect and didn't care if their POWs got sick or died.

Other countries, like the United States, treated prisoners far better. After the war, the Japanese commanders and the prison camp guards who had been so harsh were brought to court and often sent to jail.

Everyone waiting knew that the enemy forces would most likely treat them horribly, and many suspected they would lose their lives. Judy stuck close to Les and remained silent.

On March 17, Judy, Frank, and the rest left behind in Padang were officially taken prisoner by the invading Japanese army.

In the race to escape, they had fallen just short of the finish line.

CAPTIVES

The next day, March 18, the Japanese took stock of their prisoners. The first thing they did was to separate the women and children, who were put into their own internment camp. Then the men were sectioned into four groups—British, Aussies, Dutch, and officers of all nationalities—and marched through town to the main Dutch army barracks. Roughly a thousand men took part in this humiliation.

The men felt all eyes upon them. Their defeat was complete. They were dirty, ragged, washed out. The soldiers among them felt unworthy of their code of honor. The civilians wondered how things had gone so wrong. There was no love along the route for any of them. Dust from the streets swirled in their faces, the Japanese guards prodded them with their rifle butts, and the locals snickered behind their backs as they passed.

Peter Hartley, a young Royal Army sergeant whose memoir, *Escape to Captivity*, detailed his imprisonment, felt the eyes on him and felt the shame well up. But national pride kept him and his friends from caving in. "The knowledge that we were British...acted as a goad which forced our heads up and made us march with almost the precision of guardsmen. Even the wounded fought to overcome untold agonies, rather than falter in their step and be humiliated by being abused or kicked by the guards."

Upon arrival at the Padang barracks, the prisoners were confronted with hundreds of hysterical women. These barracks had been the main shelter for the wives and children of native troops in Padang. Now they were being forcibly removed from the rooms for defeated Westerners, those who had previously lorded their "superiority" over the locals. Their protests were mixed with the crying of their small children and the screaming of the Japanese, who slapped, kicked, and clubbed the families out of the building.

Judy, whose dealings with these strange shouting soldiers had included a formative kick in the stomach when she was a pup, likely gazed upon the violence and found her hatred of these men, so different in attitude and even scent from her friends, reinforced.

When the local families had been fully evicted, the POWs settled into the barracks. Each group of 250 had a one-story building to themselves, set in a rectangle around a large common courtyard that was big enough to house a soccer pitch. The men became familiar with their surroundings and settled into a kind of routine. There were a gymnasium, wraparound verandas, and an old recreation area, complete with billiards. A Ping-Pong table offered the chance for regular tournaments. J. A. C. Robins, who had survived the *Grasshopper* bombing, later wrote about winning "twenty cents prize!" after coming out on top one day.

A POW named Anthony Simmonds kept a diary of his internment at Padang, recording his activities in a pocket day planner in small, slanted handwriting. In this journal he tersely set down the daily routine, which included "[wakeup] 545, parade [presenting themselves to be counted] 615, breakfast 840, lunch 1240, and another parade at 430 followed by tea at 5 pm. & lights out at 930." The men were on their own for food after dark. Mornings included cleaning of the barracks and the heavily used showers (Simmonds took three showers a day), and, often, an afternoon nap.

81

There was no thought of mass escape—most of the men were too run-down, and the thick, deadly jungle prevented anyone considering an attempt from actually trying. Besides, life in the barracks wasn't all that bad. In addition to relative luxuries like showers, billiards, and Ping-Pong, there were dorm rooms and large converted spaces that housed the men comfortably.

Frank lived in the enlisted British main quarters. Judy, following her nose to where there was more food, took up mostly with the officers, including Les. As such, she didn't encounter Frank in this prison, which was a pretty large place, with lots of prisoners and places to roam. Judy was no stranger to any of the four main barracks, but if Frank caught sight of the dog at Padang, he never mentioned it in later interviews.

While it might seem strange to some that the two never crossed paths in the enclosure of the barracks, it isn't too far-fetched. Les and the others who came in close contact with the pointer kept quiet about her for the most part, for fear she would be killed. And Frank himself seems to have been something of a loner.

Remember, Frank lost his father at a young age. He was still a boy in many ways, just twenty-two years old, with little in common with the seasoned infantrymen and salty-dog sailors in his midst, especially those from other countries. Frank was thrown in among men who had killed others, either from a distance or up close. All he had done in the war was fix broken radar systems. He was a bit of a dreamer, still the youngster who had lost himself in the idea of flight, and an introvert, not one to call attention to himself or strike up a conversation with a stranger, even with little else to do.

He was, in short, someone in need of a good friend.

PRISON

Had any of the POWs known what was to come, they would have appreciated the Padang compound for the comparative paradise it was.

It was, after all, a beautiful place, with the towering green mountains providing a scenic backdrop beyond the gates of the prison. There was none of the backbreaking labor that would later define their imprisonment. They played marathon bridge and other card games on the veranda in the mornings, slept away the brutally hot afternoons, and played soccer matches in the evenings—which sure beat being shot at or bombed.

Believe it or not, one of their favorite things to do

was... schoolwork! With nothing else to do, the POWs spent a great deal of their free time studying. They learned Dutch, because there were so many people from Holland in the camp. But Greek and Latin were popular languages to learn, too. (*Canis* is the Latin word for dog, which is why dogs are called canines.) They also studied math and talked about great books.

Almost every day the men held lectures that were well attended. Robins wrote of attending a fascinating "talk by Miller on insects." Simmonds recorded in his diary almost every seminar he attended. "We went today to hear a lecture on the original invention of the sound track in cinemas," reads a typical entry. Others included lessons on tin mining, math, bookkeeping, and business, along with "the trials and tribulations of being a bus conductor—quite amusing." Funnily enough, given his situation, Simmonds even took in a lecture on sailing.

The Dutch prisoners felt especially at home, since they practically were. Most had been living in Padang when the Japanese came, and they had houses nearby. So their families were able to bring them things from home, like mattresses, furniture, and, most important, money. With the cash, they bought food from native sellers who were allowed to do business in the camp and through the gates. Many Dutch even went over the walls at night to return home, a practice that became so brazen that the Japanese had to threaten to shoot one of every four POWs should anyone escape. "In retrospect I doubt whether the threat would have been carried out," remembered John Williams, "but in view of other atrocities perpetrated by the [Japanese], it was certainly taken seriously."

Because the Dutch got to do things like go home at night and buy good food from the local markets, the other prisoners started to really dislike them. This feeling worsened as the food supply dried up for everyone else. Yes, the conditions at Padang weren't that bad for a prison camp, but when the men started to get really hungry, it didn't matter much. Brits like Frank and Les had lost everything when they were sunk by the Japanese while escaping from Singapore. They had no money to spend and nothing to trade. Since the Japanese hadn't begun work projects, the prisoners weren't earning anything, either. So the food peddlers working the barracks were just teasing them.

"By force of circumstances," Hartley wrote later, "the Dutchman found himself in the position of [being rich and powerful] in a new society, while the British [and Aussies] constituted the downtrodden masses." The Dutch and Brits argued furiously over who was more to blame for being in jail. "At least we fought in Malaya and didn't allow the [Japanese] to take the bloody place by telephone," one English sailor said.

So scrounging around for scraps of food became the norm for most of the non-Dutch POWs. They rummaged through trash heaps, stood outside the Dutch barracks hoping for handouts, begged and pleaded with the vendors for something to eat, and stole as much as possible.

Dogs spend much of their time sniffing around for yummy treats, so Judy fit right in. Most of her day was spent foraging for food. She was quite an accomplished predator. Rats, snakes, lizards, insects—she killed and ate anything and everything she could find. She also was a gifted partner of the men who swiped food from the locals. She made it a point to accompany Les, Jock, and a couple of other thieves on "Market Snatch Day." Once a week there was a day when all the local sellers could come right into the camp and set up shop. The penniless sailors would browse around and make a big show of picking out specific goods. One of them, usually Les, who was fun and loud and liked to joke around with people, would noisily haggle with the seller, distracting him or her while Jock and the others stuffed their pockets with food. There was also a scam in which one prisoner would pick up and inspect a large load of foodstuffs and "accidentally" drop some. Judy would swoop in, grab the food, and deliver it to a waiting Jock, who would disappear in the crowd.

In another episode, someone from the group lured a goat that belonged to the Japanese officers to the British compound, using banana peels. The goat followed its nose, sniffing out sweet banana smells, until it was outside the barracks. Another sailor, watching from a window, managed to slip a rope around the animal and haul it up to the prisoners, who cooked and ate it right away. They then spent a long night getting rid of any evidence, even the poor goat's hairs. The Japanese commander, furious, ordered a search of the entire barracks block, but nothing was found.

Judy, being Judy, enjoyed visiting the other barracks, especially the Australian one, as she had made friends with the *hancho*, or boss, of the group, Sergeant Stricchino. In the Australian barracks, a manhole led to a forgotten sewage system, which allowed the prisoners to slip outside the camp. Stricchino, recognizing Judy's gift for stealth and trickery, made the pointer part of an operation of breaking and entering. The Aussies raided local homes for food, drink, and various creature comforts. Sergeant Stricchino would bring Judy along to sound the warning if anyone came to arrest them.

The Aussies flaunted everything they stole, appearing in front of their block lounging in lawn chairs and reading glossy magazines. No one could figure out how this was happening, and when the Japanese confiscated the items, the plucky Aussies always turned up the next day with more.

But Stricchino ruined the scheme all by himself. One day he asked a Dutch prisoner to translate a book he had stolen. The man, a doctor, recognized it as a medical textbook that had been taken from his own home. The doctor ratted him out. In short order, the manhole system was discovered, and after that Judy stayed away from the thieving Aussies.

But her nighttime roaming continued, which made Les and his buddies very afraid for her. There was a small hole in a mesh window of their barracks. Judy could make herself small and slip through, and she started going on raids in the dark in search of food.

Judy was very brave and seemed able to escape from any mess she found herself in. Still, it seemed just a matter of time before she would leave and never come back. The men worried she would be shot by the Japanese or the hungry local people. Les went to the Japanese officers in charge of the prison camp and told them that Judy was a full member of the Royal Navy. He argued that killing the dog would be the same as murdering one of the prisoners. The Japanese didn't care about that, though, and just laughed at Les.

Late one night, Judy came home with a half-eaten chicken, which she accidentally dropped on a snoring prisoner, a pal of Les's named "Punch" Puncheon, scaring him half to death. After that the men began keeping her on a leash at night. "This isn't punishment," Puncheon assured her, "but we just don't want you to be eaten by the [Japanese]."

ON THE MOVE

Frank and Judy spent three months in Padang, and still they hadn't teamed up. Frank kept to himself, while Judy kept out of sight. Then one day, rumors began to circulate around the barracks. The POWs were going to be moved— where, no one knew, but they figured it must be to someplace much worse. Afternoon naps and evening soccer games were no doubt coming to an end. With so much chatter, something surely was going to happen, and soon. Everyone was nervous about the future.

Finally, the word came down: The prisoners were being moved in two groups of five hundred men to the sea—specifically, to Belawan, a port city nine hundred miles from Padang. It was far across Sumatra, through the same jungle Judy had walked to get to Padang in the first place, and well north. They wouldn't have to walk this time—at least they hoped not!—but it would be a long trip into the unknown.

Soon enough the men were moved out. The Dutch tried to take their creature comforts with them, including their mattresses and furniture, but the Japanese ruled that each man could only take a single bag. That was no problem for Frank, as he didn't have a lot left. Les had a different problem—what to do with Judy?

Judy had been pretty much ignored by the Japanese so far. She had achieved this by remaining out of sight when it mattered. But to get to the new prison camp and stay with her friends, she would have to trot past the guards and take a seat on a truck. Obviously, she couldn't do that. So the prisoners decided to hide her under some rice sacks and slip her onto one of the trucks when no one was looking. She could pop out for air once inside. When the trucks came to a halt, Judy would disappear back under the sacks. A tricky plan, but it worked! When the convoy started out of Padang, Judy was safely on board and on the move.

The transport across Sumatra was grueling, five long days of sweat and discomfort. The caravan of trucks traveled through the mountain passes, at times terrifyingly close to steep drop-offs (the men didn't dare look down). When they reached the equator, Frank, Les, and the other prisoners were ordered to get out of the vehicles and walk across, then get back into the trucks on the other side. It was a weird thing to have to do, but the Japanese had some strange customs, and no one dared to argue with them. Judy was the only one to stay inside the truck.

It was in many respects a roller coaster of a journey. The days were very hot and humid, but the nights got quite cold. The men were skinny and shivered in the dark. The scenery that passed by outside the trucks was beautiful. They had some good chow, too, thanks to frequent stops at local markets. It was like any long and boring road trip—the best part came when the trucks pulled over on the side of the road and the men could get out and buy something to eat. Anthony Simmonds recorded eating sardines and "14 cents worth of bananas." A POW named John Purvis remembered years later the glory of eating a buttered roll with his legs dangling over a shimmering lake. If only for a moment, he felt like a free man enjoying one of life's simple pleasures. All too quickly, though, it was back into the truck, and the journey continued.

At last, the convoy plunged out of the highlands and down to the sea. Many of the men, even the sailors, were scared to see the ocean. After all, it hadn't been that long ago that they had been swimming for their lives, Japanese planes overhead trying to bomb or shoot them. They were lucky to have survived the water then, and now all those bad memories came back with the sight of the sea.

When they arrived at Belawan, Les and his friends carried the rice sacks off the truck. In the confusion and bustle of the offloading, when they were sure no one was looking, they let Judy slip away to hide in the dock area. There was no shortage of equipment and shadows, and she skulked around unnoticed. She had made it.

Judy's ears picked up the loud voice of a Japanese man. It was the new commander, a colonel named Hirateru Banno. He stood on a large box and told the men in perfect English that he was their father and they were his children, and they must obey him, or he would "shoot us or cut our heads off," Hartley wrote. Not much of a welcome. On a lighter note, Banno added that he hoped the prisoners would be happy in his camp, and that his fondest wish was that they would all be returned home after the Japanese won the war. Then the POWs were herded into dark and dirty one-room concrete huts.

All Frank and the others wanted to do was sleep. Judy, too, was exhausted from the trip, which had been especially hot and uncomfortable for her under all those heavy sacks. But while they could ignore the dirt and the hard concrete floors, they could not ignore the mosquitoes. In the thousands, the insects tormented the POWs. So most of the men stayed up slapping their bodies, while the dog used her leg to scratch at herself.

The group had to deal with the devilish bugs for only a few nights. Then the Japanese announced that the prisoners would be on the move again. They held their breath, fearing they were going back out to sea. Happily, that would not happen; instead, they would be taken by train about a dozen miles inland to Gloegoer, a suburb of Medan, the main city in central Sumatra.

They were crammed into steaming hot railcars, with twenty men literally sitting on top of one another, a narrow slit in the door the lone source of light and air. "My god it was hot," Anthony Simmonds wrote in his diary, "with the midday sun beating down on the metal roofs of the trucks." Most likely, Judy slipped on board the train just as she had the truck. Though it isn't known for sure exactly how she made it aboard, she did, and was soon panting in the fierce heat, her tongue hanging out of her mouth. The trip was short, fortunately, and soon men and dog blinked at their new home as they stepped off the train.

It was June 27, 1942. Earlier in the month, the Japanese momentum in the Pacific had been blunted at the Battle of Midway, where the aircraft carriers that were spared by not being at Pearl Harbor pummeled their Japanese counterparts; in North Africa, the German general Erwin Rommel's Afrika Korps had taken Tobruk, like Singapore another British military stronghold; the Germans had pushed deep into Russia, driving for Stalingrad and the large oil fields to the south; and General Dwight D. Eisenhower had just arrived in London to take command of the Allied war effort (see sidebar) in Europe.

THE ALLIED POWERS AND THE AXIS POWERS

The United States and Great Britain fought on one side of World War Two. Japan and Germany fought on the other. But both sides had many other countries fighting alongside them. The United States fought along with the Allied Powers, a group that included the British Empire and the Soviet Union. Their opponents were the Axis Powers, which, in addition to Japan and Germany, included Italy.

Germany and Italy joined together first, signing a treaty called the Pact of Steel in 1939 to formally agree to fight together. Japan came aboard in 1940, signing what was called the Tripartite Pact, which declared that the three countries were on the same side.

The Allied Powers came together to oppose the Axis, especially when the Germans began invading other countries. The United States was part of the alliance, but for a number of years only sent weapons and money. It wasn't until Japan attacked America in 1941 that the United States formally joined the Allies.

Both sides had numerous countries that provided either soldiers or equipment to their cause. China, naturally, fought against the Japanese and with the Allies. Others who supported the Allies

And worst of all, the Nazis were carrying out their horrible plan of killing huge numbers of Jews and others they considered unworthy of life. They called it the Final Solution.

The POWs knew little about any of this, however—at the moment, their world was limited to the collection of native homes and Chinese shops that made up Gloegoer, a small outpost on the main road into Medan. Here, too, was an old Dutch army barracks, known as Gloegoer I, which was where the POWs would be held.

This ugly and grim spot was Frank's and Judy's new home. It wasn't very nice, but it would become a special place for the two best friends.

GLOEGOER

For Judy, Gloegoer was a much harsher setting than Padang. The food was even scarcer. The guards were tougher and more hostile. Her friends were weaker and more distracted by their own suffering.

Think of everything Judy had been through already—the sinking of the *Grasshopper*, the stranding on the desert island, the punishing jungle trek across Sumatra, and the capture and imprisonment in Padang. Naturally, she was exhausted. She had lost weight and energy. Before the Japanese took Singapore, Judy had weighed about sixty pounds, but now she weighed less than fifty. Her fur coat had gone from a deep, rich brown over white to more faded shades. And anyone who looked her in the face could see that those once-soft brown eyes were now harder and not so welcoming.

She still had yet to meet Frank, although he sometimes saw the dog ambling around camp. So when they first got to Gloegoer, Judy stuck close to Les, Punch, and the other friends she knew best. She slept near them, often hidden under bunks or in the shadows at the ends of the barracks. The guards at Gloegoer began to see her about more and more, and while some of them didn't care, others tried to kick her flanks or hurl stones at her head. Judy generally was too quick for them. Still, she didn't like having to dodge rocks, so she learned quickly to stay out of sight when possible.

But it wasn't always possible to lurk in the shadows. Hunger, and the need to hunt for her meals, drove her into the open, especially in the spaces between the barracks and the fences that surrounded the camp. She could slip through those fences easily enough and dash into the forest, where she could hunt for food. Getting past the guards who patrolled near the fences was the tricky part. Judy began hunting mostly at night, when more animals were out and the guards were more easily avoided.

Despite her limitations, Judy loved being around the men and found ways to have fun with them. Anthony Simmonds wrote in his diary about exercising the pointer. "Much amusement this evening caused by racing the dog Judy up and down the 100 yd barrack block; even used the kerosene food tins as hurdles for Judy to jump over."

From the moment a Japanese sailor punted Judy across a Chinese street when she was a puppy, Judy had disliked the Japanese she encountered. In this camp, where the guards were more visible and aggressive, she appeared to take those bad feelings to a new level. "She always loped with her eyes on the guard and her lip curled upwards in a silent snarl," Les recalled, "and her obvious hatred put her life in constant danger from a rifle bullet."

Fortunately for Judy, many other things distracted the guards at the prison, so for much of the time she was forgotten. But her friends were also active, much more than they had been at Padang. The men were sent off on work details that took them away from Gloegoer for the entire day. When in the camp, they foraged for food with increasing desperation. There wasn't much time left for proper dog care. The POWs who had grown to love her, whose lives Judy had saved on the desert island by finding water and leading them across the Sumatran jungle, were upset that it had become hard to return the favor. They consoled themselves by noting that Judy had proven herself a

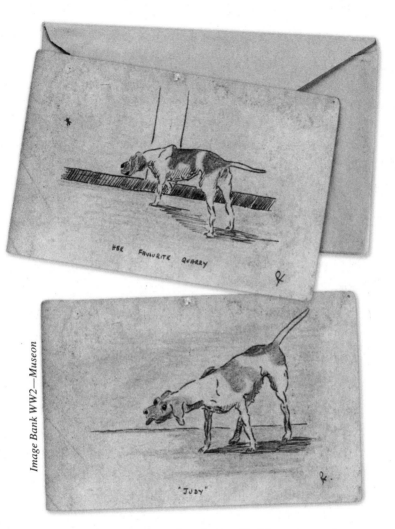

Several POWs took note in their diaries of Judy's presence at the Gloegoer camp. One prisoner even took the time to sketch her.

Image Bank WW2—Museon

survivor many times over. If there was ever an animal the men would feel secure about leaving on her own, even in an enemy prison camp, it was this most resourceful pointer.

The camp itself was much less attractive than Padang, which had mountains and the nearby sea. At Gloegoer, except for a few coconut palm trees, there was nothing but dust and dirt. The barracks where the men lived were over-crowded, dirty, and hot. Each building where the prisoners slept contained two long raised platforms separated by a central concrete gangway. The beds were nothing more than wooden planks, six feet long and eighteen inches wide, on steel girders.

The tiled roof was infested with rats, which scurried about frustratingly out of reach, though Judy would sometimes snare one. Only one side of each barracks had windows. There were three barracks to hold the Dutch, one for the Brits, and one for the Australians. All were crowded into an area barely bigger than a football field. They were "very cramped," according to Simmonds. "There were 199 of us in one building and 120 in another," J. E. R. Persons wrote in his diary. "Each room intended for 80 [workers] not 199. . . ."

Each man's bed space was his castle, where he slept, played cards, ate, talked to his friends, read books, lay ill with malaria, everything. He had another prisoner eighteen inches away on either side. *Privacy* was not a word that carried much meaning for the captives. There were shower and toilet facilities at the end of the barracks. A POW named John Hedley recalled that the toilets "were an open drain that you squatted over and hoped for the best." Holes in the wall led to gullies outside the building that flushed away the dirty water to the sea.

There wasn't much free time, but when a prisoner had a moment, he could visit the camp library, which the men built themselves over time. A large number of famous works of literature were available, including the complete volumes of William Shakespeare, Ernest Hemingway's *For Whom the Bell Tolls*, *How Green Was My Valley* by Richard Llewellyn, and—no doubt a favorite for Les and the other navy men at the camp—the Captain Horatio Hornblower novels. These books by C. S. Forester told the stories of a brave and smart British sailor in the nineteenth century's Napoleonic Wars who rises through the ranks to become a legendary captain, even though at first he gets terribly seasick. The stories inspired the TV (and later movie) adventures of Captain Kirk in *Star Trek*, so you can imagine how the prisoners fought over these exciting tales, reading to escape their terrible reality, if only for a few minutes.

But then the men had to go to work.

HUNGRY AND TIRED

The POWs had other ways besides reading to keep their minds sharp, though the daily lectures that were available at Padang had stopped. At Gloegoer there were trivia contests and spelling bees, with teams representing the air force, navy, and army competing for prizes that almost always involved food. After winning one such contest, Simmonds exulted in his diary, "By Jove that fruit salad was good." The men also enjoyed playing bridge, a complicated card game that requires teamwork between partners. It was a good way to try to forget about how hungry they were.

Still, food was always on their minds. The POWs got their grub from two sources—the Japanese and the local sellers. The food the Japanese fed them was very poor in terms of nutrition and taste—and there was very little of it. It might sound pretty good not to have to eat much bad food, but lack of a proper diet led to sickness and exhaustion. The men felt tired and hungry almost all the time.

For breakfast the POWs received a watery rice they called pap, which was tasteless unless some banana or other fruit was thrown in. It was so gooey it was sweated out of their system within an hour. Lunch consisted of rolls, at least until the flour ran out, after which it was replaced by more rice. Dinner was yet more rice, a thin soup made from barley and tree leaves, and a mysterious meat stew called ongle-ongle. It was flavorless and slimy and looked like "frogspawn," according to one Dutch survivor. A British POW named Fred Freeman remembered that it resembled "wallpaper glue," and indeed a similar product was used in the Netherlands to stick flyers up on walls.

The Dutch cooks could usually whip up one decent meal per day for the POWs to augment the pap and ongle-ongle. Colonel Banno even allowed them to plant a vegetable garden, though once it began to sprout edible plants he changed his mind and took it all for his officers. "This caused a great outburst of wrath from all the prisoners," recalled John Purvis. "And then the Japanese relented a little and said they would not take it all but whatever we had would be deducted from our rations. So, in the end, the camp was no better off."

One of the main shortages at Gloegoer was salt, which was needed badly in the tropical heat—the nutrients the men sweated out were hard to replace. Groups were regularly organized to march to the nearest inlet and gather seawater to use in cooking. The men then filtered out the salt, in a process called distillation, as best as possible. The salt could then be used for food, and the water itself became drinkable, too.

No matter what they did, though, they were always hungry. Sleep, already difficult, turned impossible with the pangs ravaging their bodies. Their gums bled from a lack of calcium; their skin flaked from a lack of vitamin A. Their immune systems were stressed to the breaking point.

In his diary, J. E. R. Persons tracked the dwindling supply, moving from "Food is a bit short nowadays, the midday loaf is small and the evening not enough for most, though it is sufficient for me" to "There are only two subjects of discussion—food and vengeance!" and "Feel as weak as a kitten and don't know how I shall manage a day's work but the others are doing it so daresay that I shall make the grade" within a few months.

Ironically, even the one food they did get plenty of—rice—proved to be bad for them. The consistent diet of white, polished rice resulted in a disease called beriberi, which was brought on by the lack of vitamin B_1, or thiamine. The rice consumed by the POWs was dehusked during the harvest, which made it last longer but removed the vitamin. A prisoner knew he was about to get beriberi when his ankles started to swell up like balloons. Soon the sufferer would seize up from nerve paralysis, his heart would beat irregularly, his limbs would spasm, and, often enough, he'd die, unless he could get his hands on some of the vitamin, like in the form of eggs and enriched breads. While the flour lasted, beriberi (*bæri* means "weak" in Sinhalese, the language of Ceylon, and is repeated for emphasis) was rare; once it ran out, ankles swelled all over camp.

The best way to get the crucial vitamin was to buy food from the locals who set up shop in the camp and nearby. But to get money to buy food (and other things, like soap and paper) from these markets, the prisoners had to work, and work very hard.

What they had to do changed all the time. On the bright side, they got to leave the camp, usually for the entire day. Some men would go into the forest to cut down trees, whose wood was used in a variety of ways back at the camp. Frank and the other prisoners could hack away with axes at humongous trees, some hundreds of years

107

old. It was hard work, but at least the men could take out their frustration by swinging the ax over and over into a thick trunk. Finally, the tree would start to teeter, and shouts of *"Timber!"* would be heard across the woods. The men always tried to send the trees falling in the direction of the guards, hoping they might get lucky and squash one or two.

A similar job took the prisoners to an old automobile plant owned by the Ford Motor Company. No cars were being made in the big factory anymore, and the Japanese wanted the building, and all the machines inside, knocked down so they could use the materials for other things, like ships and planes. The men banged away all day with heavy sledgehammers, even though they were weak and tired from the poor diet. While it was exhausting, Frank could imagine he was hitting one of the guards, or the fences that kept him imprisoned.

At every job, the men stole as many items as possible to bring back to camp and use for themselves. Anything they came across could be put to use. A tin can could become a coffee mug. A piece of wire could be twisted into a handle for the mug. Wood planks could be turned into a stool. A hubcap could work as a dinner plate. Though the Japanese threatened beatings for prisoners who stole from work sites, all manner of loot was brought back to the barracks anyway.

When they came across electronic parts, the men stole as much as they could and built radios in the barracks. They were desperate to hear news about the war, mainly when the Japanese would be defeated and their friends and allies would come to free them from the camp. By now, they had been cut off from the real world for a long time.

Unfortunately, most of the news they got was from Japanese broadcasts, which seldom told the truth about battles, especially if they went badly for the Japanese. Newspapers hardly ever got to the camp on time, either. Simmonds recorded receiving a stack of *New York Times* from mid-1941—in December 1942.

Most jobs, though, were incredibly boring. The prisoners were forced to carry loads of wood from one end of the Belawan dock to the other, stack them perfectly, and then carry them back. They would roll oil drums across fields for no purpose. They would untangle miles of rusty barbed wire, clear pathways of weeds, unload cargo from ships, sort scrap iron. "It was purely an exercise to keep us occupied," recalled John Hedley.

The biggest work project was a Japanese temple the men were forced to build. The work was backbreaking and took many months. But when it was finished, a beautiful pagoda stood shining on a hill, surrounded by flowers, fountains, and traditional Japanese landscape features. It wasn't for them, and the work had been brutally tough, but at least the men could take pride in a job well done.

"There were few men who worked on this job who could have failed to find some compensation for their labors in the thought that here at least was something to show for many weary hours of toil," wrote Hartley. "Here was something created in the midst of destruction, something which possessed a certain beauty to those who could regard it without prejudice."

But you can't travel to Sumatra today and see this temple. Soon after the war ended, it was demolished, and the jungle retook the area where the temple was built.

JUDY AND THE SKULL

As the months went by, the food situation got worse and worse. The POWs got sicker and sicker.

At first, the POWs were surprisingly healthy, relatively speaking. But soon they came down with malaria, a disease that causes fevers and chills and is passed along by mosquito bites. They got dysentery, a stomach sickness that results in endless trips to the bathroom. And of course they were malnourished. Whenever a man fell ill, he was unable to work. The Japanese held food back from anyone who didn't work, which only made things worse—with no energy, they just stayed in bed.

Sometimes, they didn't recover. Many men died from

malnutrition and disease. One of them was a friend of Judy's named Cousens, a private who had a job making and repairing boots for the Japanese soldiers. He thus had access to leather, which he would cut off on the sly, at great risk, and feed to Judy. Leather wasn't exactly a feast—it was tough and hard to digest—but it had nutrients she needed, so Judy made the effort, chewing so hard she would have to hang her exhausted jaw over her forelegs and rest it afterward.

Cousens and Les were driven by their growling stomachs to do a desperate and foolish thing. They snuck over to the Japanese officers' quarters, ordinarily a trip to be avoided at all costs. Cousens, in his role as boot maker, had spotted some unguarded sacks of rice nearby, and he talked Les into going with him to steal them.

Stealing the rice was "surprisingly easy," as Les said, but the two men forgot about an inspection scheduled for the following day. As the guards approached the blanket where Les had hidden his bounty, he was in a panic. Discovery meant a certain beating, or worse.

Then Judy sprang into action.

"I think animals have a built-in radar system which picks up all radiations of different sensations such as fear, happiness, panic, and sorrow, as in fact postmen will confirm," Les said after the war.

Radar? Probably not. Radar is based on sound waves. Judy, like all dogs, had great hearing, but her best sense was smell. Dogs tend to see the world through their noses. It's like the way people see the world through their eyeballs. To Judy, the smell of something—like a person, a tree, or another dog—was the way she understood what that thing was, and how she should react to it.

There is a funny-sounding German word to describe the way Judy used her nose to "see." It is *umwelt*, pronounced "oom-velt." More important than remembering the word is understanding the difference between how people see dogs and how dogs see people. This is why even the family dog will smell your hand before letting you pet him or her. It's the dog's way of making sure who you are.

Judy could smell changes in attitudes from people, thanks to her special sniffer. She could sense when a friend of hers was upset, or happy, or—in this case—in danger. She would then appear on the scene to help. It isn't unusual for a dog to "smell fear." But what was rare was what Judy did when her senses were alerted.

"Judy certainly sensed the danger in that room," Les continued, "and she also knew what to do about it. She also knew, as we all did, that the [Japanese] had a deep fear, almost horror, of skeletons, graves, almost any evidence of death.

"It cannot, then, have been any coincidence that brought Judy charging into that room at that critical moment like a mad beast, her ears back, eyes glowing redly. And in between her bare teeth was a gleaming human skull!"

It isn't hard to believe that Judy would have learned that dead bodies, in one form or another, distracted the Japanese, those humans she recognized by both sight and smell. Or maybe it was just coincidence. Whatever the reason behind it, it worked. Judy completed several circuits of the room, nimbly avoiding all obstacles and the Japanese, who were hysterical at the sight of the skull. Just when it seemed a guard would have to raise his rifle and shoot Judy to quell the disorder, she dashed out of the room as suddenly as she had burst in. The guards were still all worked up from the mad dog with the skull, and were yelling in high-pitched voices. Soon, they left, too, the inspection forgotten. Judy had saved Les and Cousens from a certain beating—and she had also saved their stash of rice, which they later consumed.

Cousens wouldn't get to enjoy his victory for long, however. He fell ill with malaria and died shortly after stealing the rice. Judy would be spotted stretched out, head on foreleg, by the small area Cousens had used for a work space and where he had fed her the leather. "It was as if she was in mourning," Les said.

Judy had lost a friend, and she had also lost her most reliable source of extra food. She would now have to replace both.

JUDY MEETS FRANK

In early August 1942, Frank began to see more of the brown-and-white-blotched pointer, whom he had briefly glimpsed in Rengat. She was skinnier now, and moved a bit more slowly, but it was the same dog for sure. Since Rengat, Judy and Frank had crossed paths a few times, generally at mealtime, when Frank would often flick her a few grains of rice or, as a special treat, a maggot. The disgusting little creatures were basically baby flies—they had yet to turn into their adult form, much the way caterpillars turn into butterflies. They were all over the daily rice that the prisoners ate, and just looking into a bowl and seeing the squirmy bugs was enough to make the POWs want to puke. But Judy didn't care—she liked eating the little bugs.

Frank didn't stand out to Judy in that way, since plenty of the prisoners slipped her a tidbit from time to time, albeit no more than that—they couldn't spare the calories. But with Cousens gone and food scarcer than ever, Judy was out and about, sniffing around the other prisoners more openly. This was a dangerous move on her part because it brought her into closer contact with the guards, who wouldn't hesitate to throw her into a boiling pot and turn her into dinner. But hunger was making everyone do things they wouldn't do otherwise. Judy was no exception.

Usually, Judy tried to look around and sniff out food for herself. Geckos, or cheechas as they were called locally for the sounds they made, worked the rafters for insects. Judy would stalk the lizards for hours, as she would the rats and other vermin that were everywhere. In the fields, she devoured anything she could find and kill, from immobile insect larvae to speedy bats. She caught the odd frog but didn't like the taste, which suited the men—they captured the hoppers themselves and held races with them. But these were only occasional feasts. Ultimately, Judy was forced to make do with scraps from the men.

Frank began to take more interest in Judy than he had before, now that she spent more time nosing for food among the prisoners. He spent a day or two observing the dog as she sadly sniffed about the camp, searching for anything to eat. Frank wasn't aware that Judy had recently lost a human friend who'd fed her regularly; he just knew the dog seemed troubled and no one in particular seemed to be taking care of her.

Something wobbled in his soul. He was in a terrible situation, and it was all he could do just to survive himself. He could die or be killed at any time. But the sight of this dog wasting away, without help from any of the human friends she clearly relied upon, was intolerable to him. The friendship between man and dog, forged over thousands and thousands of years, won Frank over and pushed him to put aside his own needs and care for the animal.

So on a very hot August afternoon, Frank decided to act. After waiting on line for the usual portion of rice to be slopped onto his makeshift plate, he sat on the ground in the open area reserved for eating meals. The men were busy shoveling the food into their mouths with their hands. Judy, as usual, swerved her way around the bodies, nosing for scraps. She recognized Frank as someone who usually had some extra morsels for her and began to wag her tail. She sat down in front of him, almost at attention, as a well-trained dog will do when commanded to sit and stay.

Her watery brown eyes gazed at Frank. He poured some of the pap into his palm.

"Come on, Judy," he encouraged. "This is yours."

The pointer remained frozen but emitted a soft whine. Frank knew instinctively what she wanted—not merely food, but a friend to share it with. He put his dish on the ground and used his free hand to tousle Judy's ears and stroke her head.

"Okay, okay," he murmured. "Make yourself at home, girl."

Judy visibly relaxed and lay down at his feet. Then she vacuumed up every atom of rice in an instant.

And thus did Judy meet Frank Williams. She would spend most of the rest of her life close by his side.

BEST FRIENDS

While Judy had been very close to other humans, like George White and Les Searle, she was still her own dog. She was as much a friend to the food those men shared with her as she was to the men themselves. But with Frank, things were different from the start. It was a love story. Maybe Judy sensed how caring and giving Frank's gesture was. A starving man was going hungry so that she could eat his rice. No wonder she fell head over heels for him.

But why did Judy, who had been a close buddy of several other men, decide she would go beyond that with Frank? Perhaps, despite the fact that Judy's nose and stomach made most of her decisions, it was her eyes that sealed the deal. Frank was quite boyish-looking, especially for a soldier. He was twenty-three by now. Even after the hard times during the war, he retained his youthful appearance. In fact, even when he was a senior citizen, photos of Frank would capture his unique fresh-faced twinkle.

Frank was only six months younger than Les Searle, for example, but appeared far younger. It's possible Judy was attracted to Frank's adolescent features, even if they were sunken and drawn from hunger.

Of course, no one can ever know for sure just why Judy chose Frank to be her best friend. It's possible that at first she was just following her instincts and chose the human most likely to keep her fed and thus alive. At this point, she was in her most vulnerable state. On the *Gnat* and *Grasshopper* she had been healthy and vital, and on Posic and in the jungle her animal instincts had made her all-important. She had belonged to everyone she encountered, until now.

Now she needed the help of this friendly species more than ever, and the options were few. Frank seemed like the most reliable. She didn't hesitate to get attached to him. The dog whose very first act as a pup had been to run away from her family, and who had spent her life falling into and somehow getting out of one dangerous situation after another, finally was ready to give herself fully to someone else.

Frank was never a really emotional guy. This was a very important moment in his life, but he hardly ever talked about it. And even when he did, he kept the story about meeting his best friend short and sweet: "I decided to permanently adopt her" was the way he would put it to later interviewers. But make no mistake about it—Judy won him over from that very first meal. The dog needed him, and it seems he needed her just as much. There is no record of Frank's having been a dog or animal lover as a kid growing up, but he became one now.

Whatever happened exactly, man and dog took this occasion to seize the moment—or, more accurately, the moment seized them. Right away, the two hit it off, as if Judy had been Frank's pet for years. "I just had an immediate connection with her," Frank would recall after the war. "It was as though I could understand her every thought, and more amazingly, she could understand mine."

His connection with Judy also helped bring the shy radarman out of his shell, as Judy's popularity with the other POWs transferred to Frank. The other prisoners, who barely knew Frank, began to think that he must be cool if Judy liked him so much. Frank interacted more with his fellow prisoners, though his primary relationship was with his new dog.

Naturally, food was their main concern, so it stood to

reason that one of Frank and Judy's first acts as new best friends would be to develop a scheme to help fill their bellies. On the temple grounds, instead of flowers, the Japanese would leave fruit at the shrine. Frank taught his dog to hide in the bushes and listen for his signal as he worked. He would snap his fingers or give a low whistle when the coast was clear, and Judy would dart in and swipe the fruit, which the two would enjoy back in the shadows of the forest.

The risk they ran with this scheme became apparent when one British soldier was caught stealing in a similar manner. He was ordered to pick and eat a dozen papayas. The rest of the POWs were paraded in to watch him. The man made it through four of the papayas, then indicated he couldn't go on. He was smacked on the head and told to continue. He choked down a couple more, then keeled over, unable to control his bowels. Still he was ordered to keep eating. At last, half-conscious and deathly pale, he finished. "The [Japanese] delivered their usual lecture to us and ordered him back to quarters," remembered one prisoner. The thief's neighbors in the barracks can't have been happy with the smell.

Judy may have been a pointer who never learned to point, but otherwise, she was a smart dog and learned quickly. Faster than you can say "Judy," she recognized

123

Frank's voice, not just his normal speaking tone but the various ways he said things. She tuned into his sharp finger snaps and the tempo of his whistling as it changed from slow to fast. Her ability to learn commands was quite natural, and pointers as a breed are more receptive than most hunting dogs to their masters' voices, which certainly helped Judy in her swift attachment to Frank. She paid complete attention to her new friend's every action, no matter how subtle.

Judy's ability to elude the guards and raid the jungle for food proved important to Frank once they teamed up. Before meeting Frank, Judy would either eat what she caught in her paws right away, or bring back largely chewed leftovers for the men. Now she refused to let go of any captured rat or snake until she delivered it, often still wriggling in terror, directly to Frank. If the radarman was put off by the disgusting deliveries, he never mentioned it. More likely the idea of meat for his supper overpowered any gag reflex. He shared any extras Judy brought him with the other POWs.

Not all of Judy's training was devoted to finding or stealing food. She quickly learned a variety of tricks and games. In addition to the standard fare of sitting, staying, rolling over, and the like, Frank taught the dog to hide on command. He would snap his fingers, and Judy would disappear under a bunk, only to reappear at the far end of the barracks at a second command. Judy would stand stock-still, then tear off at full speed at a gesture or sound from Frank, only to come to another dead stop when Frank gave a different snap or whistle or nod.

Much of this was done to combat the boredom and terror of camp life. Frank would ignore his work duties, at risk to himself, to spend time teaching the dog new tricks. When they had an act down pat, the duo would perform it for other POWs, sometimes for just a few, other times in front of large groups. There was hardly any fun in the POW camps. Watching Judy scampering about performing tricks at Frank's command was a rare treat for the prisoners.

Clearly, their awful situation in the camp was a huge factor in explaining why Frank and Judy clung so fiercely to each other. But there was something deeper there as well, a rare bond that would later prove to be almost spiritual in nature. From the first, they were as important to each other as life itself.

So Frank decided to risk his life to ensure Judy's safety with a daring, almost foolish gamble.

POW #81-A

Aside from Judy, there were hardly any dogs around the POW camp. The only other dog that the men saw more than once was a scrawny, mangy mongrel they soon named Tick, as she was often covered by the insects. Unfortunately, Tick was killed by a guard, an incident that highlighted the dangers Judy faced every day. When Frank tried to stop the guard from killing Tick, he himself was beaten up.

After that, everyone figured Judy was the only dog in the area. Which made it even more amazing when Judy became pregnant with her second litter. Frank and friends were dumbfounded but became very happy at the thought of some puppies in the camp.

As with all pregnant canines, Judy was brooding and irritable in the days before she gave birth. Like a bird, she built a "nest" of branches and vines to make a comfortable home for the pups. Then she began licking herself madly. It was practice for the nonstop grooming she would perform on her pups to bond with them and, because the maternity ward was outdoors, to keep away pests. The pups were clearly coming soon.

The birth became a huge community event within the prison walls, a reminder to all that love and new life still existed in a world turned upside down. Simmonds recorded the event in his diary entry of November 18, 1942. "Judy gave birth to 9 puppies! Dr. Kirkwood and all the Dutch medical staff and supplies were at her disposal. Both Judy and her puppies are doing well!" Generous gifts of precious fruit and food were made to the proud mother, who tended to her pups as best she could in her weakened state.

Puppies are born blind and helpless, utterly reliant on their mother to live. Judy instantly forgot all about her human friends and devoted herself to her young. For a couple of weeks, even Frank was essentially ignored, though he was a regular presence at the nest.

Five of Judy's litter lived, which is almost incredible, when you consider how skinny and weak she was. And being born into such horrible conditions was no picnic for the puppies. The ones who survived were probably made from the same stuff as their mom—sheer grit and a steadfast will to live.

The pups put on weight and made it to the one-month mark, a sign they would not die of malnutrition, anyway. Simmonds wrote, "Judy's puppies are growing up fine on bully [beef] and condensed milk," this thanks to the POWs who combined their spare emergency food for the puppies. "They are very loving," Simmonds added. Alluding to Judy's mascot days, Persons recorded in his diary that "[Judy] is probably on Navy ration strength." And Simmonds later noted men "playing with Judy's lovable puppies," as did Stanley Russell, another diary-keeping POW. Russell even sketched the new mother jumping about with her offspring.

The five pups that survived were named Kish, Sheikje, Rokok, Punch, and Blackie.

Kish was the cutest and most playful of the litter. Sheikje was the most attractive after Kish, in Les's opinion. One day a native fruit vendor passed along a whispered message—the women of a nearby prison camp wanted to know if they could have one of the puppies. Frank agreed, and together they managed to smuggle Sheikje over to the other camp. The fruit vendor put the pup in her basket, covered her with several bunches of bananas, and walked out with the basket on her head. She then strolled into the women's camp in the same manner and delivered a now very sweet-smelling Sheikje to the grateful women. Years later, one of the Gloegoer POWs talked to a woman who was imprisoned in that camp as a child. She had never forgotten Sheikje and the woman who brought the puppy in on her head.

There was a small drain hole in the wall of the compound, and it was through this passage that Rokok escaped the camp. Rokok was knocked into a peaceful sleep with a whiff of chloroform and shoved through the hole to a waiting intermediary, who delivered the unconscious pup to some government officials from Switzerland, who had an office in a city a few miles away. Punch and Blackie hung around the camp, but sadly, both eventually died young. Blackie was killed by a guard, while Punch disappeared altogether, his fate unknown.

It was Kish, that cute little scampering bundle, who would play a critical role in the next stage of Judy's life.

Lieutenant Colonel Hirateru Banno was the camp commander at Gloegoer. He was sixty years old when he was put in charge. His headquarters were a group of small buildings and huts that sat a short distance from the camp. Banno had been in the army his whole life and had retired to his farm in Japan when the war with China broke out in 1937. He went back into the service but was too old to do much in terms of combat. Instead, he was put in charge of POWs captured by his military.

Banno wasn't like many of the other Japanese at the camps. He wore glasses, was quiet and respectful, and was, overall, rather decent. He didn't scream at the enemy prisoners, beat them, or humiliate them. He had a gray mustache and a pleasant, almost kindly face. He was tall, taller than most of his fellow Japanese soldiers. He liked to have a drink, or two—sometimes three. Everyone knew about it, and they also knew he really liked a local woman who lived in a nearby village.

Frank knew that this woman loved Judy. She invariably cooed "Judy, come" in her limited English when she encountered the dog, and was always trying to pet her, play with her, and nuzzle her ears. Judy was only too happy to oblige, unless Banno was standing next to her. Judy didn't like Banno. She didn't like any of the Japanese.

The Japanese didn't like Judy, either. Lately, they were trying to hurt her more and more often. Maybe they were bored, maybe they were sick of the dog, maybe they were just mean.

"The guards were malignant against Judy [they hated her] and many threats were made to kill her" was how Frank put it.

So in the early months of 1943, Frank took action. He had a plan so crazy he thought it just might work.

He waited for a day when he could be on a work detail that put him near Colonel Banno's headquarters. Then he managed to duck away from the detail, taking up a spot in the bushes near Banno's living quarters. After a little while, he saw that Banno was alone inside. It was time to play his trump card—a wiggling, drooling furry ace in the deck, the fattest and cutest of all of Judy's puppies—Kish.

Frank entered Colonel Banno's room and plopped the puppy down on a table. Banno—as usual, Frank suspected—had taken a few drinks, and he was in a pretty good mood. Kish waddled to and fro and played a game of balancing on the edge of the table, almost falling over before regaining his legs and moving toward Banno. Amazingly, the colonel roared with laughter.

"He was very drunk and seemed to forget that he was talking to one of the prisoners," Frank remembered later. "I had heard that alcohol put this normally very aggressive man in a good mood, and given enough to drink, he was likely to agree to anything."

It was time to test that theory. Frank said he had

brought Kish not just as an amusement, but as a gift. The gift was not for Banno, though. No, this dog was meant for Banno's lady friend from the nearby village.

Banno was very appreciative of the gift. He thanked Frank for his thoughtfulness. Yes, the pup would make a great present for his friend.

So with rare good feelings in the air, Frank delicately brought up the pup's mother—Judy. He talked about the risk to her life from the guards, the natives, and the crocodiles; how brave and loving Judy was; and how important she was to morale.

Then he made what seemed like an outrageous request. He wanted Banno to officially make Judy a prisoner of war, which would offer her some protection as a military servicemember and at least make the guards think twice about shooting her.

Banno thought it over for a while. Frank's compassion and care for his friend were much appreciated, Banno said, but he couldn't do it. The Japanese Army, he explained, was crazy about details, about making sure everything was in order, especially when it came to matters like the number of prisoners in a work camp. Much as Banno regretted not being able to help, he wouldn't be able to explain to the officers above him back in Singapore why there was now an extra prisoner in the Gloegoer camp. Many questions would be asked—they'd wonder, Why is there a dog in the camp at all?

Fortunately, Frank was steps ahead of the colonel and ready for this answer. "That is a simple problem to avoid," he told Banno. "Simply add the letter *A* to my number." Frank carried the prison number 81, or *hatchi ju-ichi*. By merely making Judy prisoner 81-A, she could be granted the official status without raising suspicion.

At this point, Kish, as if sensing the pivotal moment, rolled over and plopped onto Banno's hand, looking impossibly cute with his big brown eyes, a trait inherited directly from his mother. Banno simply couldn't resist the puppy. He rolled Kish over and over on the table, smiling broadly. Then something incredible happened. Banno changed his mind and agreed to Frank's request.

History had been made. Judy became the first (and only) dog to be named an official prisoner of war.

As Banno scrawled the official order, Frank looked at the puppy—and held his breath. Kish was peeing. The little pup left behind an enormous puddle, mere inches from the commandant's elbow. Would the entire plan now fail, just because Kish couldn't hold his water?

But their fantastic luck held. Banno stayed dry, as did the order making Judy a POW. Frank bowed and thanked the officer over and over, then got out of there as fast as he could.

The next morning, Judy turned up at roll call proudly wearing a specially made attachment to her collar that read 81-A GLOEGOER MEDAN. If anyone needed another reminder that this pointer was special, Judy now wore the proof on her collar. She was an official POW, and that designation acted like a superhero's shield, protecting her from the Japanese who wanted to kill her.

And she was going to need that shield soon enough.

NISHI

Not long after Judy was placed on the official prisoner list at Gloegoer, Banno was transferred to another post. In June 1944, a new commander took over. Unlike Banno, who had been relatively friendly, the new man in charge was definitely not.

His name was Captain Nishi (in some accounts he is referred to as Nissi), and from his first moments in charge of the camp, it was clear there was a new sheriff in town.

On his first day, Nishi ordered all the prisoners into the common muster square in the center of the barracks area—every single one of them, including the sick and wounded men, even the prisoners who were so ill they were about to die. They limped out or were carried out on stretchers. The sick leaned against comrades or slumped miserably in the heat. The dying were laid out in a row, not too close to any of the other prisoners, who were afraid to look at them.

Nishi stood at the center of the formation, impatiently smacking his cane on his polished boots, his uniform starched to crisp perfection.

As he watched the men assemble, his gaze fell on Frank—and then down to his feet, where Judy stood at attention. Nishi was flabbergasted. A dog! There was a dog living in the camp? A prisoner's dog! What was going on?

He stood silent, shocked beyond words, for a few moments; then he strode toward the human POW and his best buddy, the canine POW.

Frank's heart was pounding away in his chest. Judy had been an official POW now for several months. Seeing how angry Nishi was, it looked as if that was about to come to an end. Frank had to think of something. As Nishi approached, Frank was intimidated by his hard manner, so different from that of the kindlier Banno. For her part, Judy began to tremble all over her thin frame, and as usual she snarled and growled in a low tone at the approaching Japanese soldier.

Frank knew that if Nishi screamed out an order to kill or seize the dog before he could explain Judy's special status, all would be lost. Being a POW meant nothing when it came to the anger of a Japanese officer. In prison camps across the Pacific, human POWs were beaten and killed all the time. No dog would get better treatment, that was for sure. So Frank quickly fumbled in his pockets to fish out the well-worn piece of paper he carried bearing Colonel Banno's official order making Judy a POW. He held it out to the surprised Nishi, pointing at Banno's signature while saying over and over again, "It's okay, it's okay."

Nishi grabbed the precious document, and a bunch of other officers appeared, everyone examining the paper and Banno's signature. They were all confused. Why would the colonel have signed this? How had Frank gotten it? What sort of trouble would they get into for ignoring it, for killing Judy (and maybe Frank, too)?

Frank waited, his nerves screaming, while the Japanese debated. Slowly, very slowly, he moved Judy behind his knees, as if that could help if the order was given to shoot.

Frank, like all the POWs, knew the paper was mostly for effect. The unpredictable Japanese could certainly ignore it at any point. But one member of Nishi's staff thought it was legally binding. He took out a book of regulations, pointed to something inside, and convinced the commander not to kill anyone—or anything—that Colonel

Banno had gone out of his way to protect. Nishi grunted, shot a hateful stare at Judy, and stomped back to the center of the formation.

Judy was safe. Once again, somehow, she had slipped out of danger.

Nishi did have an order he could make stick, however. He sent every one of the prisoners out to the Ford Motor Company plant (the same one mentioned earlier). The men who'd been working there were supposed to have knocked the whole thing down by now, but they were behind on the job. It was a combination of being utterly exhausted and going slowly on purpose.

Now Captain Nishi gave them forty-eight hours to finish the destruction of the plant and its machinery. He threatened severe punishment to anyone who worked slowly, and a dire outcome if they didn't finish the job in two days.

The men worked until nearly midnight, when, numb from exhaustion, they were at last trucked back to the barracks, only to be awoken at dawn the following day for a return to the plant site. The punishing pace dropped dozens of men and badly weakened many more. But by late in the afternoon of the second day, the last of the machinery had been stripped down and carted away.

Nishi was pleased and told the prisoners that as a

reward for their hard work they would be allowed to sleep in. Finally, some rest!

But on the third day, the wake-up horns trumpeted before dawn as usual. When the groggy men mustered in a daze on the square, Nishi had a surprise announcement: "According to the Imperial High Command," he read from a scroll wrapped around a bamboo rod, "all prisoners are ordered moved to Singapore."

The reason behind the brutal pace of the work at the Ford plant had become clear. Nishi had been tasked to finish the job before the camp was moved, and he had done so, at a terrible cost.

Still, most of the prisoners smiled at this announcement. They were more than happy to get out of Gloegoer. Singapore might have been in enemy hands, but it was familiar to many of them. And they reasoned that it had to be more comfortable than Gloegoer. Imprisonment in Singapore meant they might at last get some letters from home, or some news about the war, which they hardly ever received in the Sumatran jungle. "Cheer up, lads," Les told a few buddies of his who had collapsed and were lying on stretchers. "You'll soon be out of this."

While the prisoners were busy packing their few things and getting ready to move, Captain Nishi himself appeared in the barracks. Frank rose from his usual spot,

139

Judy between his legs. Nishi strode over to him. His English was pretty bad, but his shouted orders were perfectly clear. Frank would be going to Singapore. Judy would not. The dog would be left behind in Sumatra to fend for herself.

It was a way to get rid of the dog without going against Colonel Banno's order. Judy wouldn't last long on her own, that much was obvious. Frank was shaken, but the clever man who had worked so hard and risked so much to safeguard his dog via official POW status wouldn't cave now. The problem was his and his alone. The other prisoners loved Judy, but Frank could hardly ask them to risk their lives over a dog, especially now that they finally had something to feel good about.

There was no way he would leave Judy behind—even if being discovered meant death for them both, which it surely would. He loved her too much.

So Frank decided on another half-baked plan. He would hide his friend, somehow smuggling her onto the ship that would ferry the POWs across the South China Sea and back to Singapore.

He had used a puppy to talk a Japanese colonel into making Judy an official POW. By comparison, this should be easy, or so he thought.

The first plan he considered was to use a brown suitcase that a Dutch prisoner had found in some remote corner of the camp. It would hide Judy easily enough, but the Japanese would rightly wonder why Frank was hauling luggage around. They would look inside, and Judy would pop out. The game would be up.

Judy had already proven that she could learn tricks and repetitive techniques, and by then she was quite attuned to the various tones of Frank's voice, the small differences among his whistles, clicks, and finger snaps. So Frank taught Judy a new trick. There were only a few hours left between lights-out and when the POWs would be mustered at dawn for their train.

They would have to hurry.

Rice sacks were as common as flies at Gloegoer. No one thought twice about either one. If Judy could be hidden inside a sack, Frank might be able to slip her into a truck when Nishi wasn't looking.

So Frank spent the wee hours of the morning teaching Judy to leap into and out of a rice sack at the snap of his fingers. He kept the snap quiet, relying on her keen hearing, because it would be useless if their signal was too loud or too obvious. He also spent some time with the sack slung over his shoulder, Judy inside. That way the dog would get the feeling of being held in such a strange position. It was dark, and there wasn't much air to breathe or room to move, but she handled it.

Of course, there was no way to guess how long she might be hanging upside down in the dark, stuffy bag. And Frank would have to hope she could hide and scamper on cue. For her part, Judy quickly got the hang of this new trick, and by the time the first streaks of light pierced the darkness over the prison camp, Frank figured his pal was as ready as she would ever be.

At dawn, the prisoners were ordered to muster. Frank made a show of tying Judy with a long rope to a pole. It looked tight, but he made sure the knot would loosen and release when pulled. "Now, you stay right here, girl," he said, a little more loudly than necessary, just in case any of the guards were watching him.

The guards counted and recounted the prisoners and checked and rechecked the sacks of rice and packs of possessions they were taking along. Frank had been in Sumatra for two years and four months. He had hardly anything of his own to take with him. But since the plan required that he be seen with and known to possess a full rice sack, he shoved a blanket into one and kept it at his feet.

The guards were satisfied. Nishi himself then walked down the lines of prisoners, checking that all was ready. When he came to Frank, Nishi looked over the prisoner's shoulder at the dog tied up behind him and smiled.

Then he gave the order to move out.

There were seven hundred prisoners left alive, down from nearly a thousand when they had made the move from Padang to Gloegoer. They shuffled and limped toward the gates. The men stared straight ahead and put one foot in front of the other, as best they could.

Frank lingered near the rear, as far from the guards as he could get. Every now and again he snuck a peek back toward Judy and was relieved to see she was watching him carefully. As soon as he cleared the gates of the camp, he whistled sharply, then coughed to cover it up, in case anyone had noticed. He also made a small motion with his arm.

When he finally dared to look back at his dog again, Judy had slipped her knot and disappeared. Frank couldn't see the pointer anywhere. Clearly, she was staying out of sight, but at the same time, Frank was worried. If any of the guards were to catch just a glimpse of her...

But then he heard a low grumble and turned to catch the sight of two familiar wet brown eyes and a black nose poking out ever so slightly from the shadows under a nearby wagon. Judy had made it.

So far, at least. Now came the riskiest moment yet. Frank kneeled down as if to tie his shoe. He whispered to several other prisoners, and they formed a loose circle around him, leaving open a narrow gap. Frank then took the blanket from his sack and snapped his fingers.

Judy bounded over from her hiding spot, zipping into the gap between the prisoners, and went straight into the sack. In one smooth movement, despite his physical exhaustion and the tension of the moment, Frank closed the sack and swung it and the now forty-five-pound dog onto his shoulder. Another man took his blanket. And without drawing any undue attention, Frank rose and stepped onto his train.

Stage one was complete.

SNEAKING ABOARD

For the moment, all was well. The train rattled down the tracks toward Belawan, a journey of about forty-five minutes. When they arrived, Frank waited until the train had almost stopped, then opened the sack and told Judy to dash for cover. One problem: there wasn't any forest that she could get to without being spotted. So the dog made a clever move. She doubled back and hid in the last place anyone would think to look—under the train itself.

The prisoners were lined up at the depot and marched the short distance down to the docks, where again all their things were checked and counted. Frank had stuffed the blanket back into his rice sack to match what he had carried onto the train. The ship they would soon board, a graying hulk, loomed above them but cast no shade for relief. The prisoners sweated buckets in the heat. No one moved except the guards, who listlessly patrolled the perimeter of the formation, just as bored and hot as the prisoners under the punishing sun.

Frank could hear nothing except the beating of his own heart. There was no cover between the train Judy was hiding under and his rice sack. How would he get Judy to cross the two hundred or so yards between them without being seen? Would he even be able to snap his fingers loudly enough for her to hear? He had thrown this plan together in a few hours, and it had always had this weak link. Now he worried it would all come undone.

Then—something was happening. Frank didn't know what it was right away. There was no loud talking, no big movement, but something odd was going on. Frank soon got the message: Judy was making her way to the formation.

Frank desperately looked out of the corner of his eye and spotted his dog creeping toward him. She was crawling on her stomach like a soldier inching into position, head low, not making a sound. Somehow she had managed to reach the edge of the column of prisoners without a guard raising the alarm.

Now Judy crept between the rows toward Frank. Not a man looked down, which might give away Judy's presence. No one spoke or even whispered encouragement. After what felt like forever, the wriggling pointer arrived at Frank's feet. Frank waited for a few moments, to make sure no one was looking at him. Then he casually dumped the blanket out of the sack, held it open for Judy to hop inside, and deftly lifted it on his shoulder.

Judy was out of sight.

Frank's exchange went unnoticed, but the ordeal wasn't over. It took ages for the ship to maneuver into position, for the gangway to be lowered to the dock, and for the POWs to board. Frank, as fate would have it, was among the last of the men to climb up to the ship. He had been out in the broiling sun, with his dog in a sack on his shoulder, not moving, for nearly two hours. It was only natural that after all this time he began to lose his strength. Sweat beaded down his back, his limbs started to shake, and his vision started to blur.

A lanky Australian man was standing next to Frank as they waited. He knew Judy was in the sack. He knew Frank was getting exhausted holding her. And he knew what would happen if Frank keeled over. So he helped in the only way he could. The man took off his wide-brimmed hat and put it on Frank's head.

"If I fall down," the Aussie whispered out of the side of his mouth, "someone will pick me up. If you fall down, you've had it, you and your dog."

Only about seventy-five men were left ashore, and Frank was one of them. The boarding continued. It had become a test of stamina. Could Frank hold out until all the men went onto the ship? Or would his strength give out?

Then he saw a Japanese guard striding toward him.

The guard eyed Frank carefully, with a hint of suspicion. He asked, *"Ino murrasini noka?" Dog not come?*

Frank looked pained. It wasn't too hard, since he was straining to stay on his feet with Judy's weight biting into his aching shoulder. He looked down at his shoes and shrugged. This seemed to satisfy the guard, who moved on.

At last, Frank's number was called. He was headed aboard, and so was Judy.

Incredibly, his plan had worked.

Frank and Judy had made it off Sumatra and onto a boat, sailing away from the cruel Captain Nishi's sentence of death.

HELL SHIP

Rust bucket. There was no other way to describe it.

The boat was called the *Van Waerwijck*. It was heavy, an anchor chain or two over three thousand tons. It was tall. It was far bigger than any ship the prisoners had used to escape from Singapore. It was gray, with huge patches of rust from stem to stern. It was as downtrodden and disheveled as the prisoners. It looked like a ship that had been salvaged from the seafloor, which in fact it had been.

Van Waerwijck had been a Dutch boat originally. It was sunk on purpose to slow the Japanese. It didn't work, and the Japanese raised it again. They threw on a fresh coat of paint and renamed it the *Harukiku Maru*.

But let's stick with *Van Waerwijck*. That was the original name, after all.

The Japanese used their new prize as a so-called hell ship. When they transported prisoners from island to island and camp to camp across the Pacific, they used these old boats. The POWs were stuffed into dark, stinky cargo holds, crushed in so tight they could hardly move.

When other countries used a ship to carry sick passengers, or defenseless prisoners, the boat was painted with a red cross so the enemy would know not to attack it. Japan didn't do this with hell ships. They didn't care if the boat was sunk. They didn't care if the prisoners aboard it were drowned or blown up. Many hell ships were attacked, blasted out of the water by warplanes and submarines. Thousands of helpless prisoners were killed by their own allies.

Over a thousand men now crowded onto the *Van Waerwijck*. There were the 720 POWs brought over from Gloegoer, and 454 more from a camp near the harbor.

The mood among the prisoners was different depending on where they were from. The Brits and Aussies were tired but happy to be getting out of Gloegoer. Many had bad memories from the last time they'd gone to sea. But life in prison was such a slog that they were willing to take their chances. They couldn't possibly get sunk again, could they?

Meanwhile, the Dutch were gloomy. They had spent most, if not the entirety, of their lives in Sumatra or the East Indies. Many were married and had families in Sumatra. For them this was a scary trip into the unknown.

The POWs reached the deck, worked their way through a narrow passageway, and then were shoved down a series of steep iron ladders into the cargo hold. Deeper and deeper into the dark hole they descended, and more and more men piled in.

The sick and wounded prisoners were jammed into pigeonholes made of bamboo racks, about sixty inches by eighteen inches, slotted in as though already in a morgue. The rest of the men clambered down, down, down. They ended up well below water level in the dark hold, scrambling down rope nets to reach the bottom. They were left breathing thick, smelly air. The hatches were then shut and battened down above them. Machinery and bales of rubber, which were more valuable to the Japanese than the POWs, took up the precious deck space. What the prisoners wouldn't have traded for the fresh air of the deck!

Frank carefully lowered his sack into waiting arms below, dropped down to the floor himself, and at last released Judy, who was gasping but otherwise seemingly unhurt by her long, uncomfortable stretch in the canvas. The two friends then pushed through the crowd to a remote corner of the hold. Judy lay there, panting, stretching, looking as bedraggled as the other prisoners.

But the dog was still with Frank, against all odds.

Peter Hartley, a young soldier who had been at Gloegoer and Padang, was nearby. He wasn't a close pal of Judy's. But like so many other prisoners, he was amazed by the pointer's bravery, stamina, and loyalty. Now he gazed with wonder at her. "I began to think dreamily about that dog," he wrote later. "What an adventurous life she had led in a few years of existence."

It was the morning of June 25, 1944. Frank would turn twenty-five in a month's time, if he lived that long. Judy was eight years old and counting. By any measure, hers had been an exceptionally eventful life, filled with fun, chaos, and heartbreak.

There was still much more to come.

The *Van Waerwijck* untied and made off into the South China Sea. It soon formed up with a convoy that consisted of three oil tankers, a pair of antisubmarine screening ships, and a minelayer. A scout plane circled overhead, on the lookout for enemy warships.

Frank knew Judy had been an old naval seadog, but it had been twenty-eight months since she had been on a boat. Concerned that the pointer would get seasick (it can happen to dogs as well as people), and worried for her well-being in the crushing heat of the hold, Frank made for the one place where there was a hint of fresh air.

A top corner platform in the stern offered not only a bit of headroom, which Frank, a lanky guy, appreciated, but also a porthole. It was just ten inches across, smaller than a large pizza, but the window could be shoved open a bit. Judy could suck in some fresh air and get a glimpse at the passing sea just below.

The old steamer chugged along slowly at just eight knots, hugging the Sumatran coast. The ship had second-rate engines, and the convoy was on the lookout for enemy submarines. The war was at a different point than when Frank and Judy had raced out of Singapore and been sunk by menacing airplanes. Now the Japanese were on the run. The Allies had destroyed a great deal of Japan's air and sea power. America, Britain, and the other Allied nations now were the hunters, not the hunted.

But the *Van Waerwijck* was also slow because it carried so many POWs. They were sweating and wheezing in the overstuffed hold. The guards above showed a hint of mercy, for once. They opened a few hatches, which let some air belowdecks. But the effect was minimal. The punishing heat and the drone of the engines lulled the prisoners to the edge of sleep. But no one was comfortable enough to actually rest.

Except Judy. She laid her head on Frank's legs and snored away the hours.

Night fell. The convoy dropped anchor and stayed in one place under the cover of darkness, only thirty miles into its journey.

A trio of POWs sat with Frank and Judy. The men had helped to shield Judy when guards popped their heads down into the hold to check up on things. The night passed uncomfortably but uneventfully. As June 26 dawned, the *Van Waerwijck* began zigzagging, to make it harder for enemy subs to draw a bead on it. The boat kept between two and ten miles off the Sumatran coast. From his porthole, Frank could see the "thick, impenetrable jungle vegetation" gliding past. Many years later, the sinister beauty of the scenery was still fresh in his memory.

Where ripe coconuts had washed ashore and had sprouted roots, the coastline was overgrown with coconut palm trees. Eighteen months ago we got to know these coastlines; the beauty of the flaming and shiny colored blossoms such as orchids; birds and butterflies with a wingspan of at least 15 cm. This was only Mother Nature's cover up. These mangrove jungles are the most dangerous and the least merciful jungles in the world, where shiny colors are used by nature as a trap to hide her true intentions. In these places a beneficent and fast death can be expected by crocodiles and snakes, or by a debilitating illness caused by insect bites.

All that morning, a handful of men at a time were allowed on deck for five minutes to relieve themselves. This was accomplished by going over the side—when moving their bowels the POWs stepped out onto a small gangplank and held on to the rail with all their strength while sticking their bottoms out over the sea. There was no toilet paper. Instead, they used a high-pressure seawater hose, usually used to clean the decks.

Eight bells sounded across the ship. In this case, eight bells meant it was noon (see sidebar). The convoy was intact, though its air cover had disappeared. Les Searle was called to the deck, where he and a few other prisoners were given the task of emptying the Japanese toilets into the sea. This was ordinarily a grim and ugly job, but the men thanked their lucky stars for it, as the work got them out of the horrible hold and into the fresh air and sunlight.

The hold was like an oven in the midday heat. The POWs were roasting. They sat in pools of their own sweat. Frank wondered if "a couple of buckets would be distributed to catch our perspiration so that we would quench our thirst." The ship had traveled about 100 miles from Belawan and was 260 miles northwest of Singapore.

At 12:42 p.m., Les looked up from his spot in the middle of the ship and uttered a strangled cry. There were no words that could capture what he saw.

It was the wake kicking up from a pair of torpedoes on the water's surface, homing in on the ship. They were coming right at him.

They had been fired by HMS *Truculent*, a British submarine commanded by Lieutenant Robert L. Alexander. *Truculent* was deep into its eleventh war patrol when the smoke of the *Van Waerwijck* convoy was sighted.

The sub stalked its prey for an hour and a half, closed to within thirty-five hundred yards, and fired its torpedoes. Alexander clearly had no idea his quarry was ferrying his own POWs. In the ship's log, Alexander noted that his target "reminded me most of HMS *Titania*, as [it] was a two deck old passenger type, painted light greenish grey and looked like a depot ship of some kind."

Later, when Alexander discovered that the ship he had torpedoed carried his fellow Brits and hundreds of other POWs, he was badly shaken. He said the incident haunted him for the rest of his life. In war, accidentally harming soldiers or sailors who are on your side is called friendly fire. Frank and Judy had both been attacked by enemies— now they were being attacked by "friends."

Both torpedoes struck the *Van Waerwijck*. The first hit just behind the wall of the port-side heating plate. In the hold, a flash of light accompanied the loud explosion; then everything went pitch-dark. Fire erupted in various

157

spots. "Corrosive substances polluted the air," according to Frank. "The shock made the boat lean over to the starboard side and while she was recovering, a second torpedo ripped the number three hold with a deafening blow."

The *Van Waerwijck* was ripped apart by this second explosion. Dozens of men unluckily close to the blast were killed instantly. The fires in the hold were put out by torrents of water that poured in through the gaping hole in the hull. Thick smoke and steam from the damaged engine room choked the prisoners. "The harsh notes of the ship's siren penetrated plaintively through the uproar," Hartley recalled.

Slowly, the air was cleared somewhat by gusts howling through the ship's wound, and Frank could make out the scene. "The light passing through the shutters made it possible to perceive the ravaged hold. The area was one big mass of bent steel and splintered wood. The only thing that could be heard was the hissing noise of the escaping steam from the broken lines and the seawater pouring in. Below us the men were trapped and buried in a hopelessly distorted pile."

It was worse beneath the hatches. The huge, heavy metal covers had blown down on top of the POWs, crushing them. Making it worse, the heavy crates on the dock broke free from their ties and, as the ship heeled over, slid down the open hatch on top of the men as well.

Between the explosions, the fire, the smoke, and the heavy stuff crashing down, the hold was a terrifying place to be for man or dog.

Frank was momentarily frozen. He was shocked by the slaughter below him. But then he felt Judy's wet nose sniffling his leg, and that "swept him back to reality." Gazing up at her friend, Judy "was incredibly calm and was motionlessly waiting for me to move." Her loyalty and instinct to keep her friends safe hadn't left her in other dire moments. Now she stayed true even as the explosions sounded and the water filled the hold.

Frank wanted to climb down and rush to safety, but the destruction made that impossible. There was no way he could maneuver through the chaos. And he definitely could not climb up and out of the hatch while carrying Judy. "In a glimpse of an eye I could see that it was impossible to carry the animal through the mess," he later said.

Instead, he turned to the small porthole above them. He could never get through, but Judy might be able to squeeze out. Not stopping to consider the consequences, Frank opened the porthole as far as it would go, picked up the pointer, "shoved her head and front paws through the hole and commanded her to 'swim!' 'Out you go old girl!' I yelled."

Judy "looked down and back at me with a sad look. I immediately understood her: she thought I was nuts! Then she wrenched herself with curled up rear paws through the porthole. The hole was just wide enough and with a last push she disappeared from sight."

The drop to the sea was about fifteen feet.

"How Judy landed in the water must have been an amazing sight," said Frank.

He didn't stick around to try to see it. He had to save himself.

Along with several men in the area, including Hartley, who had watched Dobson climb out a porthole much as Judy had (and had witnessed Frank pushing the dog out), Frank began to clamber over and under the mess. It was a cruel obstacle course made up of twisted steel and broken wood.

And human bodies, both dead and alive.

"After what seemed an eternity," Frank and the others reached a spot directly beneath an open hatch. There was a rope ladder, but it was "besieged by a mob of panic-stricken and desperate men," Hartley recalled. Instead, they climbed on top of a mountain of smashed crates. The summit still left them a few feet from the deck. "It was

160

now or never," Hartley recorded. They all jumped for a handhold at the same time.

Frank remembered later that he was able—somehow—to grab on and pull himself up. He was exhausted and weak, but sometimes desperate situations make people incredibly strong. Because falling meant agony and very likely death, he found the power to get up to the deck. Hartley was several inches shorter than Frank, though. He couldn't manage. Agonizingly, he hung on by his fingertips. "Tears of hopelessness welled up into my eyes, blinding me."

Then, a miracle.

A hand from above reached down and pulled the struggling Hartley on deck. Several hands, actually, belonging to Les and the others in his toilet-dumping group. After the torpedoes hit, Les had found the rope ladder and lowered it into the hold. Then he and the others lifted as many as they could from the depths of the hold before the onrushing waves could sweep them all into the water.

Once again, they were all swimming for their lives in the South China Sea.

"As far as the eye could see, the sea was filled with wreckage being dragged away by the fast currents," Frank remembered. "Somewhere in there, Judy was swimming."

And so were sharks. Frank was terrified they would race to the scene and grab him—or Judy—for lunch. A few sharks were around, but they mainly fed on the dead bodies, which were easier to catch.

More explosions rocked the ocean. Two other ships in the convoy were struck by torpedoes. Frank watched transfixed as one "fish" (military slang for torpedo) zeroed in on its target:

> *A tanker sailing at full speed was hit on its starboard side. The torpedo was apparently aimed low, because the hull above the Plimsoll trading mark [a line on the hull beyond which cargo could not be loaded, so as to prevent overstuffing the hold, as the Japanese had done with the POWs] did not show any visible damage. With the prow down, the tanker plowed to the deep and sunk in a couple of minutes. It reminded me of a submarine performing an emergency dive.... Towards the [Japanese] crew of the ship I did not feel any compassion when they went down.*

Another tanker exploded in a "blinding sheet of flame," according to Hartley, "leaving no trace that [it] had ever existed." Oil covered the sea in an enormous slick. Hartley's face was so blackened that his friend, a New Zealander he called Mac, didn't even recognize him. Still,

Mac pulled Hartley from the water and onto his over-crowded raft.

A Japanese warship zigzagged to avoid being hit while randomly dropping depth charges (antisubmarine explosives), adding to the noisy mayhem. Scout planes arrived overhead to toss down bombs in an attempt to flush the *Truculent* to the surface. That just made things louder and more chaotic. The sub had disappeared.

Frank glided down the steeply angled hull of the *Van Waerwijck*, which was "loaded with mussels," and began swimming as hard as he could. He needed to escape the ship's suction when it sank. Otherwise, he would be pulled under and might drown. He had been a good swimmer since his merchant navy days, but he was exhausted. He flipped onto his back to watch the *Van Waerwijck* go under, sunk for the second time in the war. "An imposing fountain sprayed in the air because of the exploding kettles [steam pipes] and the escaping steam," Frank remembered. He was glad he had swum away from the ship so quickly.

Frank could see land in both directions. Sumatra was one way, and Malaya was the other way. The water wasn't very deep for the ocean, only about sixty feet. But that was more than deep enough to drown in if he wasn't careful.

As the sun dipped toward the water, the Japanese warship gave up hunting the submarine and lowered its

163

life rafts. But the Japanese were only interested in rescuing their crew from the *Van Waerwijck*. Any POW who tried to get aboard was kicked in the head with a boot or smacked with a pistol butt.

The prisoners would just have to keep swimming.

Frank spent two hours paddling around, desperately searching for Judy while others grabbed hold of floating wreckage. "She remained without a trace," Frank recalled. "A Dutchman that held on to a rubber bale told me he had seen Judy swimming about. At that moment I knew she still had life in her."

Three hours went by. Finally, rescue vessels arrived, a handful of tongkangs and a tanker that had been part of the *Van Waerwijck* convoy and had scurried away when the attack started. Frank was pulled on board the tanker.

"I was still thinking about that submarine," Frank said. "Was it still lurking somewhere to strike again?"

Some men recognized Frank and told him they, too, had seen Judy swimming through the wreckage. That was a shred of good news, but the scene on the tanker was grim. The deck was covered with the wounded and the dying. "They lay groaning," wrote Hartley, "and for the most part unattended, in pools of their own blood." A lone doctor, himself about to keel over, did his best without any medicine to offer the suffering survivors. He begged the

Japanese crew to take them to Sumatra or Malaya. They could be at a proper hospital in a few hours. But the Japanese refused. The crew had been ordered to Singapore, and that was where they were going. The trip would take almost two days.

As night fell, Frank, Hartley, and the other rescued POWs had a nasty surprise. The steel deck became freezing cold to the touch. The men were either naked or barely dressed. An icy wind whipped across the open space, made worse by the boat's speed. They had been on the verge of heatstroke that morning. Then they'd been torpedoed. Then they were either badly hurt or soaking wet, or both. Now they were freezing.

"The night seemed like it would go on forever," Hartley recorded. "The curses of the men who were thankful to be alive at all contrasted with the groans of the wounded who wished they could die."

Several men indeed died in the night. They were thrown over the railing and into the sea at dawn. When the sun reappeared, the deck heated up again. It was like moving from a meat locker to a coal oven. The steel got so hot the men couldn't stand on it.

The tanker steamed the rest of the distance to Singapore. Frank, nearly broken by the ordeal and filthy with oil and smoke, scanned the waters for Judy. He was a shell.

He couldn't even cry. Hartley, too, was numb, "bereft of all feelings except an unquenchable desire for a cup of hot sweet tea."

Finally, the tanker arrived in Singapore. They were back in the same harbor they had escaped from two years earlier. Frank hadn't seen the place since evacuating aboard the *Tien Kwang* as the city burned behind him. Singapore still carried scars of the invasion, but much of the damage had been fixed, and the docks appeared to be in good shape. No ambulances stood ready to carry the wounded to the hospital.

Frank got off the boat in a dazed shuffle and helped to carry men more severely wounded than he. "Japanese sailors and local stevedores stood goggle-eyed on the quayside" at their appearance, Hartley wrote. Many of the POWs had been badly burned in the torpedo explosion, others broken by falling debris.

Frank hoped desperately that Judy would be waiting at the harbor.

But Judy was nowhere to be seen. She hadn't made it.

Frank's best friend was gone.

Frank was numb. He allowed himself to be herded onto a truck, which headed to the city center. They were going to yet another prison camp, this one called River Valley.

There was little left to keep Frank alive. As another POW put it, Frank was "headed for the end hut."

When the truck arrived at River Valley, Frank hopped down and was led to the gates of his third prison camp. After nearly two and a half years of captivity, it was his lowest moment yet.

RESCUE DOG

But Judy was still alive. And she was unsinkable.

The last time Frank had seen her was when he'd shoved her out of the porthole. According to various witnesses, Judy fell into the sea and popped up, stunned but alive. She began to swim strongly, her head well above the water. Les caught sight of her right away, seeing a man with his arm wrapped around Judy's shoulder, struggling to keep his head above the waves. "Why don't you shake him off?" he yelled out, as much to himself as to Judy, for she was too far away to hear him. Surely she would be drowned by the weight of the man.

But she wasn't. She guided the man to a large piece of floating debris, and though he was totally spent, he managed to haul himself up onto it. Judy stayed in the water, looking for others to help. And help she did. Several men were seen to have been rescued by Judy, and there may have been more beyond that. In each case, the method of operation was the same. The men were thrashing about. They were tired, or wounded, or both. They couldn't save themselves. Out of the blue came Judy.

The men would hang on to the swimming dog, who would pull them to safety. Each time she approached a rescue boat, hands reached out to pull her from the water. Each time, she pulled away from them to stay in the ocean and continue saving people.

When at last there were no more men alive in her vicinity, she allowed herself to be pulled into a boat. "She was more dead than alive," recalled one of the men who witnessed her coming on board. "She had totally given herself to the drowning men."

Thanks to Judy's efforts, many men lived to see the end of the war. But even so, 178 people died in the sinking of the *Van Waerwijck*.

Judy had been torpedoed. She had been bombed from the air. She had survived countless deadly encounters with the prison guards. She had fallen overboard into a fast-moving river. She had been slashed by a crocodile. But her enormous heart was still beating.

After being pulled from the ocean, Judy couldn't relax. The tongkang she was on carried a few Malay crewmen and several rescued prisoners. A sail was turned into a makeshift shroud to cover their bodies. When the tongkang approached Singapore, several Japanese boats sailed out to meet it. Fortunately, one of the prisoners remembered that Judy was, as far as the enemy was concerned, still supposed to be back in Sumatra. Hurriedly, he pushed the weary dog under the sail that hid the dead, and she wasn't spotted by any of the Japanese who looked into their ship.

When it reached port, the prisoners were mustered into rank. Just because their transport had been sunk, it didn't change the fate of the survivors. They were still headed to the River Valley prison. Judy scooted into the crowd, looking for a familiar face. She soon found Les, but Frank was nowhere to be seen. He had already been put on a truck for the camp.

Les, however, was overjoyed to see Judy and kept her close to him. In the confusion, she managed to remain unseen until the moment Les picked her up to load her on his truck. In better shape, Judy might have remained hidden underneath the vehicle, only to dart aboard at the last moment. But she was totally spent, and Les had to risk lifting her himself.

"Tomaru!" Halt!

The sudden scream of rage came from the mouth of the last person Les or Judy wanted to see—Captain Nishi.

Nishi had been waiting patiently on the dock as the survivors of the sinking trickled in, ticking off exactly who had lived and who had died at sea. It was his job to ensure that the transfer of the Gloegoer prisoners to River Valley went off without a hitch. The sinking was a factor even Nishi couldn't account for. But he wasn't about to give up.

Then he saw Judy.

The dog he had ordered left behind on Sumatra was here, soggy and exhausted but very much alive. Her usual sidekick was nowhere to be seen. But the animal was clearly headed toward the new camp.

Nishi bellowed another order, and two guards cocked their rifles, yanked Judy from Les's arms, and brought her to Nishi. They threw her on the ground at his feet. Judy looked awful. She was gaunt, oil and muck covered her from nose to tail, and her cracked lips were pulled back to reveal yellow teeth, a parched tongue behind them. Her red-rimmed eyes glared in hatred at Nishi, who stood angrily above her.

Then came a scream.

"Nishi!"

Everyone turned in the direction of the voice. It was Colonel Banno, the Japanese officer who had made Judy an official POW. He was now based in Singapore. He had heard about the sinking and had come to the dock to meet survivors. Hartley remembered seeing him as the burned and broken passengers arrived at the dock. "His smile gave place to an expression which was surely the nearest any Japanese we had met could ever get to horror."

Banno saw Judy, and Nishi, and the colonel got very upset. Banno rushed to action. He yelled at Nishi that the dog was an official POW, and that he himself had signed the order giving her protection. Had Nishi not read it?

Yes, Nishi began, *but I ordered her to remain in Gloegoer....*

Banno blew up. This was the army—no soldier ever questioned or ignored a superior's orders. This was what made Banno upset, far more than anything about actually saving the dog. Whatever his reasoning, Banno had saved Judy from Nishi once more.

Les took the opportunity to scoop Judy up, climb quickly into the truck, and bang on the cab window. The truck left the dock with a rumble, while Banno continued to dress down the disobeying Nishi.

Once again, Judy had slipped free of danger.

But what had happened to Frank?

RIVER VALLEY

Singapore looked much different than it had the last time Frank and Judy had been there. For one thing, it wasn't burning. No planes were dropping bombs. No artillery shells exploded. The Japanese had rebuilt much of the damaged city and were now occupying it in brutal fashion. They called it *Syonan-To* (Light of the South). Many Chinese people lived there, and they suffered horribly under Japan's cruel rule. Over nearly four years, tens of thousands of ethnic Chinese were massacred by the *Kempeitai*, the Japanese secret police. One woman named Madam Wong Len Cheng, who survived the rampage, said, "Sometimes we feared even having a light in the house, for fear it might attract a Japanese soldier to enter our home." Food was hard to get. Schools were closed down. The press told the story of the war entirely from Japan's viewpoint.

The River Valley prison camp sat near the center of the transformed city, along the west bank of a quiet stretch of the Singapore River. The "valley" was formed by a narrow drain that ran through the center of the camp area. The camp itself was, if possible, even uglier than Gloegoer. There were some very old buildings, most of them just roofs and beams with no side walls. The thatch used for the roofs had blown away on several of the structures, leaving them open from above as well. Some of the two-story huts had sleeping berths ten feet or so above the ground, but the ground platforms were so disintegrated that it left the men roosting like birds.

The men looked even worse than the camp. Their faces were coated in dirt, grease, and smoke residue. Their hair was caked in sweat and salt water. They were unshaven, hollow-eyed and hollow-chested, scarred across their often naked torsos. They all needed a bath. Maybe a few baths. Many were still in shock and totally spent.

Upon arrival at River Valley, Judy refused to follow Les into his hut. Instead, the pointer circled the camp many times, looking for Frank. She went into every hut, every pen, even the toilets. But he wasn't there.

She was alone.

Judy settled down on her belly just inside the front gate and waited. Her sad brown eyes scanned everyone who came in.

Frank's truck had stopped on the way to River Valley for supplies in a native village. So although he had left before Judy got to the dock, he arrived at the camp well after she did.

Frank staggered off his truck and through the gates.

Judy saw him right away. Hallelujah!

She raced up to Frank from behind and flattened him. "When I entered the camp, a ragged dog jumped me from behind with a great amount of force, flooring me," Frank remembered with a smile. "She was covered in bunker oil and her old, tired eyes were red." Somehow, some way, man and dog had been reunited.

Frank was in tears when he finally got up from where Judy had knocked him down. "C'mon, old girl, and stop acting so daft," he said. Frank was being his usual quiet, reserved self, but he was very moved at seeing Judy again. Moments before, he feared all hope was lost. Now, with his best friend miraculously back at his side, his hope was renewed, his determination to survive restored.

"His shoulders seemed to re-set," said Les later.

Peter Hartley and Phil Dobson had a similar reunion at

River Valley. As with Frank and Judy, the last Hartley had seen of his close friend was when he was working his way through a porthole on the *Van Waerwijck*. Hartley was an early arrival at River Valley, and he paced nervously as scores of POWs were trucked to the camp, waiting for his buddy to be one of them. He began to question why he had even bothered to fight to live. "So many of my friends had perished.... Why did I not give up when I had the chance, instead of making the struggle to survive?"

At last, after a sleepless night of worry, a truck carrying thirty prisoners arrived. Dobson was among them. "It was not until we were smiling joyfully into each other's faces and gripping each other's hands that I realized how great had been my sense of loss," Hartley wrote. "From now the outlook seemed to be so much brighter, as though a world of tarnished silver had been suddenly and miraculously polished."

Frank, Judy, Peter, and Phil were the lucky ones. A lot of people they knew from Gloegoer hadn't made it out of the sea.

Now that Frank and Judy were together again, they took a look around their new home. It was a dump. But there were some friendly faces, at least. Other prisoners were already living at River Valley. They were mainly

176

POWs who had been held in Java and transported to Singapore. Most assumed they would be moving again soon.

The Java men were, like the Gloegoer group, mainly Dutch and Brits and Aussies, but there were at least a few Americans. The most notable of the bunch was George Duffy, a young merchant seaman whose ship had been sunk by a German raider. Captured and held by the Nazis, he was then traded to the Japanese and held prisoner in Java for nearly two years before being shipped to River Valley.

Duffy, like all the other prisoners, had few things to call his own. Almost everyone in the camp had been sunk at sea at least once, with everything they owned now at the bottom of the ocean. So even basic items, like eating utensils, had to be made from scratch. John Purvis remembered, "[I] managed to find a flat piece of tin which I bent into a plate and also a coconut shell which I cut in half and used as a mug. My spoon was made of a piece of bamboo."

After living in the Sumatran boondocks, they had hoped Singapore would bring them closer to civilization. But they were disappointed. There was no mail, no Red Cross. If anything, there was less food, for the prisoners at least. The entirety of their diet consisted of small balls of rice and some dried fish and seaweed, "which both looked and tasted like dried rope," according to Hartley. The men stripped leaves and bark from the trees to supplement their meager rations, but that did little to stave off the constant rumblings of their stomachs and the rapid spread of beriberi.

They were at River Valley for only a few weeks. Then rumors began that they were headed back to Sumatra. Since Singapore wasn't much better, there wasn't a lot of complaining about that. All the men knew at first was that there was a special mission back on that island. It had something to do with farm work, apparently. Maybe a harvest. Only the fittest would be allowed to make the journey, those who passed a test to prove they were still in decent condition.

The test was a big joke, though. The prisoners were lined up in groups of ten at one end of the compound. They were then marched at bayonet point to the other end. Everyone who made it without collapsing was "fit" enough to join the traveling group. The Japanese were just pretending to care about the men's health. They wanted every able body they could get.

The POWs were sent on the march once more, right back down to the harbor. This time they were loaded onto paddle steamers, like the riverboats that still head up and down the Mississippi. These steamers were slow, but they had two things going for them. One, they didn't have cargo holds like the hell ships, so the men would at least be in the fresh air. And two, no enemy sub would bother to attack them.

Judy was smuggled aboard once again, but this time it was easy. The Japanese didn't seem to care. Maybe that was a warning sign.

The dog didn't look good. She was skinnier than ever, her faded coat hanging off her body. She stuck close to Frank as the boat sailed away, and once again Singapore disappeared behind them.

This time, Frank and Judy's boat made it across the water without being sunk. They turned at the mouth of the Siak River and headed inland.

When the boat stopped, Frank and Judy splashed ashore at a muddy camp in the center of Sumatra. They were near a village called Pakan Baroe. At the edge of the camp, train tracks ran off into the jungle. Everyone from the boat boarded a train and click-clacked off into the dark forest.

It wasn't a long ride, just a few miles. The men got off and were told to march farther down the line. Judy disappeared into the brush and followed Frank at a short distance. Soon they came to a ravine. It was fifty yards wide, and way down below, there was a fast-rushing river. To fall into it would almost certainly mean death. Instead of a real bridge, there were some wooden logs with boards connecting them. And there were no handrails.

The men (and dog) crossed over, terrified.

Being held in a prison camp was bad enough, but this was something else. They were out in the wilderness with hardly any protection and very little energy left.

They were all extremely vulnerable.

Once they got over the "bridge," they walked about seven miles deeper into the jungle. Somehow, they found the spirit to sing as they went, songs like "Roll Out the Barrel" and the popular soldiers' protest song "Bless 'Em All." But soon they fell silent. The towering forest cut off all light as the sun went down. Swamp gas boiled up all around them, shrouding them in mist. Tongues swelled from thirst as the guards shoved them forward. Judy walked gingerly along, staying even with Frank's shuffling pace.

Up ahead, dim campfires lit the trail. At last, they stopped at a clearing deep in the remote jungle. They had arrived at their new home. The pitch-black night obscured their frightening new reality. But not for long.

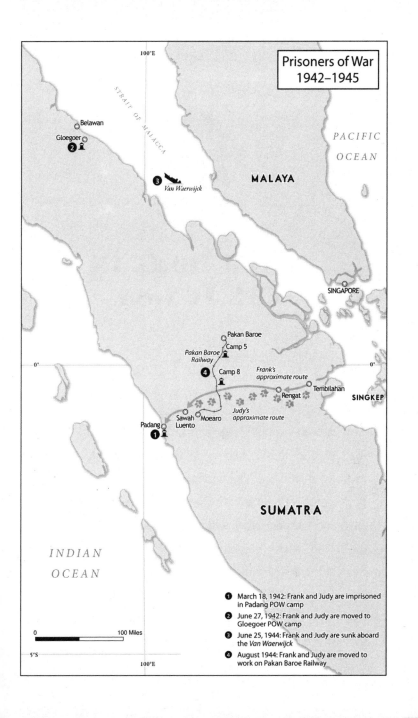

Prisoners of War
1942–1945

STRAIT OF MALACCA

PACIFIC OCEAN

Belawan
Gloegoer ❷

MALAYA

❸
Van Waerwijck

SINGAPORE

Pakan Baroe
Camp 5
Pakan Baroe Railway
❹ Camp 8

Frank's approximate route

Tembilahan

SINGKEP

Rengat

Sawah Luento
Moearo

Judy's approximate route

Padang
❶

SUMATRA

INDIAN OCEAN

0   100 Miles

5°S

100°E

❶ March 18, 1942: Frank and Judy are imprisoned in Padang POW camp

❷ June 27, 1942: Frank and Judy are moved to Gloegoer POW camp

❸ June 25, 1944: Frank and Judy are sunk aboard the *Van Waerwijck*

❹ August 1944: Frank and Judy are moved to work on Pakan Baroe Railway

A NEW HOME IN
THE JUNGLE

The rumors about farm work had been dead wrong. Instead, the POWs had been brought back to Sumatra to build a railway. The Japanese planned to link several large cities—Padang in the west, Palembang in the southeast, and Pakan Baroe, which lies near the exact center of the island. There was already track between Padang and Sawah Luento, as the POWs well knew, having ridden trains on that route years earlier, back before they were taken prisoner. That line ran farther east into the interior, to a village called Moearo.

The initial stage of the Japanese plan was to build a railway between Pakan Baroe and Moearo. This way those two places and Padang would be linked. That sounds easy enough—except it meant they would have to lay track over roughly 140 miles of dense and deadly Sumatran wilderness (about the distance between Washington, DC, and Philadelphia).

Actually, the Japanese wouldn't do it—the POWs would.

The plan was to have gangs of workers establish field camps in the jungle. From there the men would cut down trees and saw them into sleepers, the wooden ties that connect the rails. They would then lay them on the predetermined path (over, around, or through whatever natural barriers happened to be in the way) and drive steel nails to join the wooden planks to iron girders and form recognizable train tracks.

It would be an incredibly hard job even for healthy, well-fed, energetic workers. For the prisoners like Frank, it would be pretty close to a death sentence. The only good thing about the job was being outside in open spaces. Remember, they had been mostly cooped up in prison camps for more than two years. But they were beaten down, nearly naked, with hardly any resistance left.

One POW who worked with Frank and Judy on the

railway said, "Much freedom of movement was afforded but only a minimum of human dignity."

Frank and Judy woke up that first morning on the railway at their new home, known only as Camp Five (there would eventually be around a dozen camps). It was near a speck on the map called Loeboeksakat, about fourteen miles out from Pakan Baroe and a shade under six from Camp Three, which housed a large number of British POWs, including Les Searle. They finally got a look at the camp in the light of day.

Image Bank WW2—NIOD

The living conditions in a Pakan Baroe camp.

It didn't look good.

As a fellow POW in Camp Five recalled, "One look was enough to dampen the stoutest spirits." Several large huts stood close to the rail line. Scary dark jungle loomed all around them. They were in the middle of nowhere.

At its busiest, roughly one thousand men worked out of this camp, half Dutch, half British and Australian. "We worked all hours of the daylight," remembered Fred Freeman. "There were no rest days or anything."

There was no electricity—light was provided by homemade lamps that were pieces of rags set ablaze and floated in a tin of coconut oil. The roofs and walls of the huts were merely palm leaves wrapped around poles. The POWs slept on wood platforms eighteen inches wide that ran the length of the exterior, with bare earth in the center of the hut. Nature owned this space, so the weeds and grasses also grew through holes in the platforms, totally unchecked. "Rats used to run up and down over our heads at night," wrote one POW, Ken Robson. Insects were everywhere, flying in the men's ears, crawling on their legs, chewing on them in bed. The stench of rotting vegetation permeated the huts. Bullfrogs croaked incessantly from a nearby swamp.

The lack of food had been a major problem at Padang, Gloegoer, and River Valley. On the railway it was a dire threat. The prisoners, now turned slave laborers, received barely enough food to keep a resting man alive—and these men would have to perform very hard physical work.

Breakfast was the familiar, disgusting glop called ongle-ongle. Lunch was a cup of rice—leveled off with a stick to ensure that everyone got the same amount—plus a cup of watery vegetable soup—a ladleful of grotesque brown liquid that congealed as it cooled. The evening meal was generally the same as lunch, plus whatever the men could forage while out in the jungle at work. "This was little enough to get excited about," one POW remembered, "but there was always a chance some meat might be present." All of it was washed down with green tea or boiled swamp water.

"We tried to supplement the minimal daily diet in every possible manner with everything that was eatable, such as tubers, leafs, snakes, rats and sometimes even monkey meat," Frank remembered. Everything that could be caught or plucked was on the menu.

That meant fish, salamanders, insects, and lizards, as well as nuts, berries, mushrooms, flowers, green leaves, and even bark stripped from trees, which Fred Freeman said tore their stomach linings. "We used to take tin cans with us to collect jungle vegetables on the way to work," he added. "This entailed quite a risk, as if the Japanese caught us, woe betide us." To give their meals just a little flavor, they dumped handfuls of chilies into the food. Forks, plates, and cups were improvised from small pieces of zinc and tin or whatever else could be found.

It was impossible to get enough to eat. "We were all perpetually, agonizingly, hungry," Peter Hartley recalled. "Every organ in our bodies seemed to send out messages of pain, demanding to be fed. Our stomachs felt bruised and our knees trembled; we lived from meal to meal with a dumb hopelessness, knowing that even when the meal had been eaten the pains and the cravings would remain only partially and momentarily dulled. The food had as much effect on us as a short shower after a prolonged drought has on a garden. It did no more than wet the surface."

Not having enough food was bad enough. But what they did get usually made the men sick. Diseases of the stomach and bowels, like amebic dysentery and round-worm, were ruthless and gave them diarrhea all the time. It was always gross, and sometimes was truly revolting. One POW found out he had been infected in a most gruesome manner. "Harry suddenly shot up," recalled his friend Ken Robson, "sat on the edge of the bed boards and gave a cough. Putting his fingers in his mouth he produced a long worm, about as thick as a pencil and some ten inches long."

Robson explained how bad the dysentery was for the

men's minds as well as their bodies. "With no control over bodily functions there was not only the pain, but the humiliation of not being able to control oneself... the self-disgust at your own inability to prevent it."

Meanwhile, the policy of reduced rations for the sick continued. So men who felt bad couldn't eat enough to get energy from food. This meant it was impossible to fully recover. As a result, many sick men played tough guy and refused to admit they were ill. They worked and worked and worked until they collapsed on the side of the tracks, left there to tremble until their fellow prisoners carried them back to camp at day's end. The Japanese told the men that if it were up to them, sick (and thus dishonorable) POWs would get no food at all; the half-rations came as a result of the emperor's mercy.

Through it all, Judy suffered alongside the men.

While Frank slaved away for twelve, fourteen, sometimes sixteen hours on the railway, Judy stayed in the brush nearby, running around and playing a potentially deadly game of hide-and-seek. When a guard looked her way, she would duck behind a tree or lie flat in the dirt. If she was out in the open and Frank sensed a guard was coming, "I only needed to click with a thumb and middle finger or whistle softly," he said. "It was our language of understanding which she understood perfectly and without hesitation obeyed." Judy's amazing ability to communicate with Frank kept her safe.

"The simple instruction 'go away' was enough for Judy to disappear," Frank said. "She calmly remained waiting, sometimes even for hours on end, until she received my signal to reappear. This didn't save her once—it saved her many times from certain death."

Judy had transformed from a gentle "people dog," a ship's mascot who spent most of her time on the water, into a wilder animal capable of survival in untamed jungle. It was quite remarkable. "She wasn't that tame, obedient dog anymore," Frank noted. "She was a skinny animal that kept herself alive through cunning and instinct."

With her nose attuned to this new environment, foraging was her main role, both for herself and for Frank and his friends on the line. She would catch snakes and rats for the grateful men, who would add the meat to their minuscule evening rations.

When she wasn't looking for food or hiding from other animals, she would simply lie in the brush and wait for the signal to rejoin Frank. While some other camps were more open, the rail line extending from Camp Five was mostly hemmed in by trees and bush. Deep shadow was everywhere. So Judy could keep her eyes on her best friend while remaining utterly invisible to whatever guard was nearby. "Another danger came from the local population," Frank recalled, but there again the remoteness of their work site was an advantage. "Luckily she rarely came into contact with the inhabitants, because there were only a few villages near the railroad."

One prisoner named Tom Scott, who was close to the two best friends, gave this account of the relationship between man and dog:

I was always fascinated at the complete understanding which existed between Frank and Judy—they were truly an amazing team. Judy was no longer a dog that anyone in his right mind would recommend as a suitable household pet. Thin, half-starved, always on the prowl, her eyes only softened when Frank touched her or spoke to her, or when she looked up at him. Whenever she found herself too close to one of the guards, her lip curled back in a snarl, and her eyes seemed to glow with almost a red glare.

Sometimes this sort of thing would lead to trouble, and when a guard threatened to retaliate, Frank would click his fingers and Judy would disappear into the nearby jungle. We didn't see

her and didn't hear her, yet the moment he gave a
low whistle, she'd reappear at his side as if from
nowhere.

That this tactic worked so well is difficult to believe. Frank would see a guard, give a signal, and Judy would duck into cover and remain unseen. And this happened several times a day for a year. It's so amazing that even a few men who survived Pakan Baroe but never witnessed Judy and Frank in action didn't buy it. One of these non-believers was George Duffy. "I don't know how it's possible," he said. "I can't imagine any animal living more than a day in that jungle. I only survived because I was tough and I was young. No dog could have done the same."

But one did.

Duffy's doubt, in the face of many eyewitness accounts, only highlights just how astonishing Judy's story of survival was.

And things were only getting worse.

DANGERS

Judy's ability to remain alive would seem to indicate that the guards on the railway were a slack, easily duped bunch. In fact, nothing was further from the truth, making her consistent skirting of danger even more remarkable.

Some of the Japanese guarding the POWs were very cruel. One unsmiling officer had a trick. He issued orders in fast, guttural Japanese—and when the POWs naturally failed to understand whatever was being said, he beat them up. Another guard enjoyed hurling tools such as axes and machetes at the prisoners, then demanded that the prisoners pick up the implements and give them back to him.

But the main source of fear along the railway was not the Japanese—it was the Koreans.

Surprisingly enough, Korean guards were plentiful on the Pakan Baroe railway. Overall, they were much more violent, cruel, and unpredictable than the Japanese, who mainly mistreated the POWs by starving them and working them till they dropped.

At the time, Korea was not really its own country. It was a colony of Japan. In Korea, the Japanese owned much of the earth that the Koreans farmed and lived on. Most of the food went to the Japanese landowners, and they collected rent, making Koreans tenants on their own land.

Naturally, the Koreans didn't like this setup.

When World War Two started, Korean men were forced into the Japanese fight. Nearly five and a half million Koreans either donned the uniform of Imperial Japan or were sent to work in factories in the home islands. They were told they would have to serve for only two years, and would be part of economic development projects.

Instead, they were given jobs the Japanese didn't want to do.

The Korean soldiers who were forced into prison guard duty were frustrated and hated their jobs. They hated their bosses, the Japanese, but couldn't do much about that. So they took out their bad feelings on the POWs wherever they encountered them.

"The Korean guards were the most abusive," wrote a soldier named Eugene C. Jacobs in his memoir, *Blood Brothers*. "The Japs didn't trust them in battle, so used them as service troops; the Koreans were anxious to get blood on their bayonets; and then they thought they were veterans." Earlier in the war, another railway had been built by prisoners, this one in Burma (now Myanmar) and Siam (now Thailand). Many Korean guards had been stationed there. The POWs were very afraid of them but also made fun of their stupidity, calling them "moronic," in the words of one survivor. Many of these same guards were moved to Sumatra when it came time to build that railway. "Those hardliners cared not if we lived or died," wrote George Duffy.

The Korean guards were often drunk and always sadistic. They were forever face-slapping, rifle-butting, or shovel-whacking prisoners. That was just part of the average day, meant to hurry along workers not moving fast enough, or merely to vent some frustration. When the Koreans got truly angry, the punishment got much, much worse. For example, POWs were typically forced to hold branches or beams overhead for hours in the broiling sun. If they dropped their arms, the beating was ferocious.

The prisoners gave the Koreans nicknames: the Bully,

Baby Face, Flower Pot, Fat Lip, Four Eyes, the Prizefighter, Fat Porky, Black Panther, the Slime, John the Slapper, the Elephant, Cross-Eyed, Slap Happy, Howling Monkey, the Battaker, Farmer's Son, Wild Bill, Horse Face, Tapioca Jim, the Dead End Kid, Neurotic, the Basher, Rubber Neck, the Wrestler, Gladys, the Aga Khan. Some of the nicknames were funny, but they didn't make the guards any less terrifying.

One has to wonder how Judy could possibly have survived the wrath of these tough, angry men with guns. The Koreans could pretty much do what they wanted to the prisoners, including hurting or killing them. They had no regard for dogs (other than as food—dogs are regularly eaten in Korea) and saw Judy as a four-legged mockery, a skinny, brown-and-white taunt aimed directly at them. Any of them would have killed the pointer at any moment, if they could have managed it.

But several things worked against them. First and foremost was Judy's astonishing ability to disappear right in front of them. This was coupled with her sharp sense of brewing trouble, which always allowed her to bolt into the shadows before things got really bad. The fact that the jungle was huge, dark, and scary worked for Judy. The guards hardly ever wanted to chase her into the bush. Who knew what else was out there? And as Frank pointed out, "because the guards were regularly being relieved, she had the luck that her assailants never remained too long nearby."

It's also helpful to take the point of view of the Koreans. As mentioned, the average Korean guard was a man brought against his will to a place far from home, with a terrible climate much different than his country's. This guard was caught up in someone else's war, one he didn't understand, didn't care about, and didn't actually fight. He took orders from a hated member of an army that dominated his country. The tigers and mosquitoes didn't care who was a guard and who was a prisoner. The railway building project itself was ridiculous, a monumental effort to shove a man-made transportation system through miles and miles of untamed wilderness. Even if it was by some miracle finished, certainly none of the Koreans would ever ride on it or enjoy it. The only time they got to express themselves was when they beat up a defenseless prisoner.

In short, it was a bad job, held by angry and frustrated men.

So the fact that a dog was running around may have not seemed so strange. Certainly, the guards had more important things to get upset about. And there were other animals around, too, ones much more dangerous than Judy. The camps in remote areas kept bonfires raging all night to keep the big game away. Tiger droppings and elephant dung were regularly spotted. Elephants were a constant thorn in the side of the railway builders, not because they charged or tusked the men, but because they trampled the tracks, smashing the beams like matchsticks and twisting the steel rails.

George Duffy twice saw footprints that reflected the enormous size of what moved through the jungle darkness. Near Camp Five he saw a tiger print in the soft earth that was "as large as the palm of my hand." Near the end of 1944 he saw elephant tracks that "measured from the tip of my finger to the elbow. He had cut quite a wide swath through the jungle, too."

On at least two occasions, tigers got into the camps and stole food, once taking some hogs the Japanese were keeping for a special occasion. The POWs laughed at that one—it served the Japanese right. But then they were warned not to leave their huts at night except in pairs. This was particularly hard on the sick men, especially the dysentery cases. A man who needed to relieve himself at regular intervals in the night now had to wake up a friend who was fast asleep just so he could accompany him to the bathroom. And the men feared for their lives with every crackle in the bush.

Once in a while, a POW used the threat of the tigers for

his own gain. One Dutchman named Jan De Quant, who was missing a lung thanks to a Japanese bullet he'd taken during the defense of Sumatra, was great at roaring like a tiger. Thanks to his bad lung, he sounded just like one of the big striped cats. One night, he roared as loudly as he could, and the Japanese and Korean guards reacted as he'd hoped—by fleeing to their huts in terror. De Quant then slipped unnoticed into the guards' compound and stole one of their chickens, a theft then blamed on the "tiger."

It's difficult to say that tigers were Judy's biggest worry. Her instincts made her very afraid of them, but she had to find food in the jungle, and that was much more important. Certainly, Frank was worried sick for Judy. "My main concern for her safety was when she went into the jungle, due to the presence of tigers in that thick vegetation. The Sumatran tiger is a big and silent killer," he said. "Although Judy was clever and quick, she would not be a match for this jungle inhabitant in his natural environment."

Elephants were less scary, though still dangerous. But one of Judy's best moments of the war came thanks to an elephant—a dead one, anyway. Night had fallen when Frank heard his pointer "growling in the brushwood." Frank got up to investigate and came upon a surprising sight. Judy was hauling the biggest bone he had ever seen, one "as big as herself." When she looked up to see Frank, she dropped it, grinned madly at him, and started digging furiously at the ground, attempting to bury the humongous bone. It was the leg bone of an elephant. The animal's decaying skeleton was scattered over a few hundred feet of bush.

Judy soon gave up her digging and began gnawing away on the bone, a femur, or thighbone, which was about three times her size. "Go ahead and enjoy it, girl," Frank muttered. After she'd gone hungry for so long, the huge treat must have tasted like the finest steak.

Most days weren't as good as that one.

ESCAPES

Working on the railway at Pakan Baroe was agonizing for Frank, Judy, and the rest of the POWs. But somehow, all that suffering also had a bright side. They were much more open about the friendship, even love, they had for each other.

"The tenderness shown to mates who were ill, almost without exception, was remarkable," Ken Robson wrote. "When a man was ill and couldn't eat, his pals shared his food, when they were ill he had theirs. It was wonderful to see a man trying to force his sick pal to eat something, even though his whole body was crying out for every scrap he was offering after a hard day out on the line." Another

POW noted, "Hunger tightened the bonds even as it weakened the body."

Amazingly enough, the human spirit rallied, even in such totally bleak conditions. As Robson wrote, "Faith is the greatest reservoir of energy...and faith in the future was something most of us had and was unexplainable." A prisoner named Rouse Voisey remembered that he "put his trust in his comrades to come and get him out of there, and they did."

Something else brought the men together—Judy's ability to survive despite the incredible odds stacked against her. Today she might be called an emotional support animal. Even men in other camps, like Rouse Voisey, got some extra energy and good feelings when word was passed down the line of another of Judy's wondrous escapes. "We all knew of her existence, even when we didn't actually see her in action," he remembered. "It was a great thing to know someone was taking care of her, and that she was—somehow—still alive."

Judy's mere presence on the railway lifted the spirits of men who had been pushed beyond the brink. Her effect was captured by an unknown poet who wrote about life at Pakan Baroe:

> *They would stagger to their workplace*
> *Though they really ought to die*

> *And would mutter in their beards*
> *"If that (dog) can, so can I"*

Frank practically broke his back chopping down trees, carrying heavy steel rails, and hammering in nails. He could barely move after a long day on the railway. But he also had an extra duty to perform at all times—looking out for Judy. As the calendar flipped to 1945, the pointer became even more aggressive toward her Japanese and Korean tormentors. Whereas before she would zip away from their kicks and do her best to hide, she now often confronted the guards, not caring about their guns. She would snarl and growl and stand her ground, even in the face of shouts, bayonet thrusts, and drawn rifles. She would crouch just a foot or two away from the boot that had just missed her, teeth bared and eyes flashing red. Only Frank's ever more urgent whistles would get her to retreat into the bush.

All dogs started out as wolves many, many years ago. Now Judy seemed to be embracing the good old days, acting like a wild wolf, and that made her more frightening. But it also put her life in greater danger.

One day, Judy's attitude almost made her a casualty. Work was proceeding as usual on the railway when one of the prisoners dropped a piece of equipment down a small ravine. He might have done it by accident, or he might have

202

done it on purpose—no one is sure which. It doesn't really matter. The guards were going to beat him up either way. One took a long bamboo rod and started whacking him over the head.

It was hardly an uncommon sight, yet on this day, Judy snapped. When the prisoner fell backward under the assault, the pointer dashed in from the jungle. Frank had not said anything, or whistled, or snapped his fingers. Judy was acting on her own. She began barking fiercely and snarling at the guard. The guard kept his cool and very slowly, never taking his eyes off Judy, lowered the bamboo to the ground and exchanged it for his rifle, which lay ready at his feet.

Frank was scared and shouted quickly, "Go, girl!"

Judy saw the rifle flash, and she dodged out of the way in the nick of time. Frank took a few blows from the guards after the episode, then got back to work. A little later, when he had moved down the railway and judged that enough time had passed, he called to her. Judy appeared, shaken and looking "abashed," in Frank's words.

Another time, the men had returned to their huts after the evening meal when a guard began beating up a prisoner. Judy got between them and actually rammed the guard with her body. Enraged, the guard chased after her. "Disappear!" Frank screamed. He later recalled that Judy "crawled through the hole in the wall of our barracks made out of palm leaves, and she was gone." All Frank could do when Judy was alone in the jungle was lie on his bunk, hold his breath, and hope.

Night fell. Gloom settled over the hut.

Then Frank heard a shot ring out.

"Fearing the worst," Frank slipped outside and set out to look for his friend. "I crawled through the brushwood to find Judy," he remembered. "After a couple of minutes she appeared."

As he examined her, Frank's hand came up red. There was a streak of blood on her shoulder. Indeed, the bullet had broken skin, but the damage could have been much, much worse. It was a miracle. Frank covered the gash with palm leaves so the wound would not become infected. Quite literally, Judy had been an inch from severe injury or death.

But this was Judy, and she had survived so much in her nearly nine years. A near miss from a bullet was just another escape from death.

In both these incidents, Judy's interference meant that the prisoner who was being beaten up was forgotten about by the guards. The clamor of her barking and the guard's shooting at her had saved these men from a horrible flogging, or worse. They would be added to the growing list of prisoners who could say Judy had saved them from harm.

The POWs wanted to reward Judy for her bravery. They got together that night in the hut to discuss how to do that. But they came up empty. They simply had no extra food to give her, no gifts, and no extra energy to do something special for her. All they had was the hope that they would soon be liberated, and that she would somehow survive to see freedom.

DARK THOUGHTS

It was now the summer of 1945.

The lack of food and endless work had wasted Frank away. Judy wasn't much healthier. They were nearly unrecognizable.

"Judy became a walking skeleton, a shadow of what she had been," Frank said. The two of them were sharing a handful of rice per day at this point—just enough to keep themselves alive. Judy was too exhausted to hunt for more than short periods, badly reducing the food she could catch. Frank dropped an alarming amount of weight. He remembered that he weighed but "36 kilograms" at his lightest, or a shade under eighty pounds. He was basically a walking skeleton, too.

"Not one of us was fit to crawl out of our blankets and certainly not fit enough to work for ten or twelve hours on the railway," remembered Tom Scott. "Judy was scraggly and bony. Frank was down to about half his weight—just as we all were. They were both, however, mentally strong and alert. They were both steel-tough and courageous, and between them there was a complete bond of understanding and affection."

That was the only thing keeping man and dog alive.

Many others weren't so fortunate. They didn't have a best friend to keep them going. Men died by the hundreds.

At first, Peter Hartley was upset when other prisoners died from sickness or starvation or exhaustion. But it started to happen so much that "eventually death lost the power to move me." Thousands of POWs were experiencing the horror by the railroad, and they mostly felt the same way. The men's bodies were damaged, but so were their minds. "Apathy threatened to break the mental resistance, inevitably ending in death," Frank said. "In the course of time this process had taken place with hundreds of men."

Frank did have a secret weapon to combat this apathy—a furry bag of bones with brown eyes and a cold nose. Years later, Tom Scott would testify to their unshakable bond. "Frank and Judy were never apart. Where Frank went, so went Judy. They lived for each other, and I dreaded to think what would happen if either of them fell seriously ill. Both, I felt sure, would die. . . . Without Frank, Judy would have died in any case—of a broken heart."

Sometime that summer, probably in June, Frank fell seriously ill with malaria. He had been suffering mildly with the disease for some time, but this case was much worse. People with malaria switch off between burning fever and shaking with chills. The disease remains scarily persistent across the world, because it is so easily spread by mosquitoes. And Frank didn't have any medicine to help him fight the malaria and get better.

He was, for the first time, sent off the railway and into bed. Judy managed to follow him to the camp, where he lay helpless, sweating and shivering. Many other sick men went to the main hospital at Camp Two, but Frank stayed out in the remote jungle. This was a break—in the big hospital, Judy would surely have been seen. In the forest, she could hide easily enough. But she wasn't totally safe. According to one account, a Japanese officer spotted the pointer and ordered that Judy not only be killed but also cooked and fed to the prisoners, "as meat was a luxury." And Frank was to be force-fed the first helping of his dead dog.

But Judy, her sense of danger on high alert, remained out of sight, and the order was forgotten.

Another escape.

Soon, however, there was a new threat to Judy, and it came from an unexpected source—Frank himself.

While he was sick, and even after he recovered and went back to work, Frank figured he was on the brink of dying. All he had to think about was his suffering—and Judy's.

"One started to wonder if it made sense to attempt to stay alive," he recalled bitterly years later. "Even if you would survive, what would the future hold? And even if there was a future, what should one live towards? Would our weakened bodies still respond to treatment if finally made available? And when would that be? Would blindness or paralysis be our fate for the rest of our lives?"

Frank started to think that slipping away into death would be the easiest thing for him. And it would be the best way to spare Judy the agony of watching him struggle with the pain and illness that overwhelmed him.

But every time bad thoughts like these came into his mind, Frank would look down at Judy. And a realization would sweep over him—his love for her *was* noble. His responsibility to stay alive and ensure that she did, too, *was* looking toward a future. And the fact that they were both still alive, despite the overwhelming odds, despite the endless agony, *was* a victory.

This was his war. He couldn't lose it now.

Judy gave Frank the strength to stay alive; yet he could

easily die of malaria or some other disease at any time. There would be nothing Judy could do about that.

"Looking at Judy," he would later say, "now a starving skeleton of a dog, I asked what would become of her when I would die. I instinctively felt that my passing would also mean her death. Maybe even starved to death, in some dark place, somewhere in the jungle."

This idea was more painful to Frank than ones involving his own death. The nights got darker, as did his thoughts. Frank began to wonder if the merciful action to take, unthinkable as it might seem, was to kill Judy himself. The idea of his beloved pointer dying without him "raised the question if there could perhaps be a simple way of killing her." It wouldn't take much to kill the dog. Simply denying her the little food she received would be enough. Or he could "forget" to whistle or speak a warning the next time a guard was onto her.

"But would I have the courage to do this?" Frank asked. "Would I be able to take this decision and even if, how? A knife or a piece of wood? Whichever way, I would have to decide quickly as long as I still had the energy to move." One dreadful night, as the inky blackness consumed the jungle canopy, Frank made up his mind to do it. He would kill Judy to spare her.

But Judy, the ultimate survivor, was having none of it.

"One way or the other, this clever dog seemed to have guessed my thoughts," Frank said. "Curled at my feet she opened one bloodshot eye, and with that one glance, she rejected all my thoughts of despair." Judy had been defying death for so long it was second nature by this point. By staying alive all this time, Judy had kept many of the prisoners going—not just Frank. Frank had wavered, but now he regained the will to fight.

"[Judy] strengthened me to hold on, regardless of what the future might bring," Frank said of that fateful night the pointer earned one more stay of execution. "We had defied so many dangers and looked into the eyes of death so often that we owed it to ourselves to hold on, in the hope that another miracle would present itself."

As the summer dragged on, the rumors started up again. But this time, the news was good—the best possible news. The war would be ending soon. Frank and Judy would be free!

If they stayed alive, that is.

Suddenly, they had even more reason to hang on to life. To die so close to the end would be the ultimate cruelty. Frank and Judy spent each day with a single purpose— to keep each other alive. Judy slept directly underneath Frank's bamboo slab and seemed to become even more alert than usual.

That was good, because she had been officially sentenced to death.

There was an outbreak of lice in Frank and Judy's camp (they had moved up the railway line and were now in Camp Eight). The tiny bugs had been feasting on the prisoners since their arrival, so exactly why the Japanese and Koreans chose this moment to delouse the camp isn't precisely known. But heads and eyebrows were shaved, and all the bedding and most of the clothing were burned. Then came an additional order, which was likely made up on the spot by the guards:

Shoot the dog.

But they couldn't find her.

The overeager guards had made a tactical mistake. Instead of simply walking over to Judy and shooting her before announcing why, they taunted Frank first, telling him all about how they were going to send his beloved dog to heaven. This gave him the chance to shout to her the warning to disappear, and she hightailed it into the bush. The guards didn't have a chance.

Judy disappeared for three days. On the first day, the guards were too busy getting rid of the lice to look for her, but on the second day, the hunt began in earnest. Several guards teamed up and began to sweep the area, looking for Judy. Up and down the railway, on both sides, groups of men with rifles hunted for the dog. The prisoners waited and fretted.

Frank could hardly believe that he was going to lose his friend at this stage, all because the Japanese had "discovered their humanity," as he sarcastically put it.

Every now and again, a shot would ring out from the bush. Frank would hold his breath, waiting for the howl of pain. But it never came. The guards might have been shooting at Judy, or some other animals, or even just shadows. Then, late on the afternoon of the second day, a guard came sprinting out of the jungle and past a group of prisoners hanging around the train. Deeply frightened, he gasped out, *"Tora!"* as he ran past.

Tora is the Japanese word for tiger.

The rest of the guards soon appeared. Hunting for the dog clearly wasn't going so well. It definitely wasn't worth getting eaten by a tiger. But Judy didn't appear back in the camp that night, and Frank was still horribly worried. He was sure he had seen the last of his best friend. And there was little doubt in his mind, or in the mind of anyone who knew him: Judy's death would surely mean that Frank would lose his will to live.

The next morning, he heard a bark.

The barking got closer and closer, louder and louder. Frank raced outside his hut to see Judy standing in the middle of the clearing, excitedly barking and leaping in circles. Judy was usually quiet unless she was challenging a Japanese soldier or had spotted danger, so it was a shock to see and hear her barking her head off in the camp. Frank was overjoyed to see her, and the rest of the camp filled with relief as well.

It took them all another moment to realize that their guards had disappeared.

There wasn't a uniform or a rifle to be seen. The sun was high in the sky, yet there hadn't been a predawn bugle. The guards usually shouted at them to get to work—but no one but Judy was heard that morning.

They had actually slept in. Judy had been their alarm clock. That had never happened before.

Then they heard a noise. It was the engine of a car or a truck. A tall, super-skinny Aussie prisoner said, "This way," and shuffled with what dignity he had left toward the sound. It was hard for him to look noble, as he was stark naked.

Judy happily led the way, barking loudly. Then two uniformed men stepped into the camp clearing. They weren't Japanese or Korean guards. They wore red berets. They were members of the RAF Parachute Regiment.

It was August 15, 1945. The great day had arrived—the war was over (see sidebar). The men and their dog were free at last.

There was much laughing and cheering. Some men

214

merely dropped to their knees in prayer. A POW named J. D. Pentney remembered the emotions years later:

> *A simple ceremony was held in the centre of camp, where the Union Jack was hoisted to the top of a flag pole, which up til then had always flown the flag of the IJA. Every heart was full as it fluttered to the top and tears ran unashamedly down the faces of some of the toughest characters in the world.... Most of my original comrades were gone and I remembered them as I had known them, previous to our capture, young, boisterous, carefree but with a marvellous spirit that never deserted them, even in the face of the worst adversity. I was 23 and felt four times as old.*

The war in the Pacific had lasted 1,364 days, 5 hours, and 14 minutes. Somehow, Frank and Judy had survived it to the end.

V-J DAY/ATOMIC BOMBS

Near the end of World War Two, Japan was losing, but not defeated. The nation was still fighting to the death over every inch of its empire. Then the United States changed the very nature of war.

For several years, America had been developing, in secret, a massively powerful bomb fueled by the splitting of atoms—the atomic bomb. The program that developed the bomb was called the Manhattan Project (even though it was based far from New York, in a small New Mexico town called Los Alamos), and it cost billions of dollars. Thousands of the world's smartest scientists worked on the bomb. They were racing to find a way to build it, because everyone knew the Nazis were also rushing to make a similar weapon.

The German effort failed, but the American one worked. The Manhattan Project built two atomic bombs, code-named Fat Man and Little Boy. There was a great deal of argument in the military and the government over whether they should actually be dropped on Japan, because the bombs were so incredibly powerful. In fact, no one really knew what would happen when they exploded. Some scientists believed the bombs would set the sky on fire.

The decision was made to use the atomic bomb so that the Allies would not have to invade Japan, which would almost certainly mean a great many people, on both sides, would be killed. Instead, Little Boy was loaded on a plane called the *Enola Gay*, and on August 6, 1945, it was dropped over the city of Hiroshima in Japan. The massive explosion killed a huge number of people, with estimates ranging between up to 140,000 and 160,000 dead. Almost as bad was a side effect of atomic blasts—radiation. That is invisible energy that comes from the bomb. Radiation is deadly when too much gets into the human body. In this case, many more thousands were killed by the radiation.

The atomic bomb was a shock to the Japanese, but they still refused to surrender. So the second bomb, Fat Man, was dropped on another city, called Nagasaki. Many more people were killed (estimates range up to about 80,000, though no one knows for sure) and this time, the Japanese did surrender. Frank and Judy were set free on August 15, the day the Japanese finally said they couldn't take any more war or atomic death. That day became known as V-J Day, or Victory over Japan Day. May 8, the day the Germans surrendered, is known as V-E Day, for Victory in Europe.

While the atomic bombs forced the end of World War Two, their creation also began a new, frightening era, in which ever-more-powerful bombs are capable of killing everyone on earth.

Australian War Memorial

Lady Edwina Mountbatten—wife of the British supreme commander in Southeast Asia, Lord Louis Mountbatten—greeting Australian POWs at Pakan Baroe as part of Operation Mastiff, the massive Allied effort to liberate and treat POWs in the Pacific.

GOING HOME

Where would Frank and Judy go after being freed from Pakan Baroe?

Singapore, of course!

Yes, the same city they had each escaped from, three and a half years before. The same city where their tearful reunion had taken place. The same city that had now been liberated from Japanese rule and was back under British control.

The two friends went across the water one more time. This time, at last, Frank didn't have to smuggle Judy aboard. And this time, at last, they didn't have to worry about being attacked from the air or beneath the waves.

They were free, but neither was feeling great. Frank was still struggling with malaria. Both man and dog were dangerously thin and weak. Arriving in Singapore, they went straight to a hospital compound that had been set up for POWs. They stayed for a month, slowly regaining their weight and strength. Many sick men were loaded onto transport planes for swift travel back home. Frank was a borderline case. His malaria was bad, but not so severe that he was put right on a plane bound for England.

That suited Frank just fine. Judy would never be allowed to fly back home with him. Frank knew this. He had to secure a berth on a ship at all costs. He was forced to "use my powers as an orator to make sure I did not qualify for transport via air"—and it worked.

One afternoon, an orderly found Frank playing catch with Judy out in the courtyard, both looking far healthier than at any time in the past few years. The orderly handed over the official papers that would send Frank back home. "To leave for England aboard the troopship *Antenor*" were the most glorious words Frank had ever read. Then he glanced at the footnote below. "The following regulations will be strictly enforced. *No* dogs, birds, or pets of any kind to be taken on board."

It was yet another hurdle for Frank and his buddy to jump over. But after all they had been through together, there was simply no chance Frank was going to leave Judy behind. It was time for one last trick.

On the day the boat was leaving, Frank enlisted four friends to help him smuggle Judy aboard. First, Judy had to avoid the military police who patrolled the docks. She did this easily enough and found a hiding place between some duffel bags on the jetty, close by the gangway. Only her nose protruded from the heavy canvas.

Frank boarded the ship and waited until the right moment. Then he signaled to his pals to come up the gangway. They distracted the two sailors in charge of letting people on board by pointing in the opposite direction, and then walked away from the gangway. Frank, who was observing the scene from the edge of the deck, whistled once more to his crafty pointer. She zipped from her hiding spot, scrambled up the gangway, and, in a blur of brown and white, raced into the waiting bag Frank carried. In his familiar practiced motion, he closed the bag around his dog and lifted her to his shoulder.

He went below right away and hid the dog beneath his gear.

All too easy.

And so it was that after nine years in Asia, Judy was on her way to England for the first time.

It took six weeks for the *Antenor* to travel to England.

It was a very relaxing time for Frank in particular. He needed the rest. He was still adjusting to life outside a prison camp. He was used to exhausting labor, intense hunger and pain, and the terror of knowing death could come at any moment. It might seem strange, but suddenly being carefree was not so easy after all that time.

Frank was still a young man, just twenty-six. By the time the ship approached England, he had put on weight and felt much better than he had in years.

No one knew that Judy was on board the ship but Frank—and one other important person. The *Antenor*'s cook had been giving the pointer loads of grub since her first day at sea. Judy had fattened up as a result.

As the ship neared the port of Liverpool, Frank knew it was time to reveal Judy's presence to the captain. Judy's first appearance on deck shook up the crew. "When she was roaming in front of me, a crew member that met us stood stiffly," Frank remembered. "Still staring in front of him he asked: 'It could be I'm just a bit groggy, but did you just see a dog pass by? And if so, how in the devil's name did she get on board?'"

The captain was angry at first. But when Frank told him about all the incredible obstacles he and Judy had overcome together, he became the dog's biggest fan. He called ahead to insist on permission for Judy to land.

One of Frank's friends who had helped distract the ship's guards at the gangway while Judy slipped on board was a fellow RAF POW named Brian Comford. His father was a big-time London lawyer. He made some phone calls, and the path was cleared. A permit was granted, and Judy would be allowed to come ashore.

There was just one problem. And there was no way around it.

All animals, with no exceptions, that arrived in Great Britain by sea or air had to be quarantined for six months. In other words, Judy would not be allowed to go home with Frank. She would be held by herself for half a year.

England did this to prevent a terrible animal disease called rabies from spreading throughout the country. Even General Dwight D. Eisenhower, supreme commander of the European theater, had to board his beloved dog, a Scottish terrier named Telek, for six months upon arriving in England to prepare for the invasion of France.

So when the *Antenor* anchored in Liverpool on October 29, 1945, what should have been an incredible moment of triumph for Frank was instead bittersweet. He walked down the gangway, Judy ranging ahead of him on a leash, her feet touching English soil for the first time. Waiting to meet them was an official of the Ministry of Agriculture.

Frank hesitated. For days, he had tried to prepare himself for this moment. But saying farewell was so tough. How could Judy possibly understand? After all the years in the jungle, surviving the torpedoing of the *Van Waerwijck*, the reunion in Singapore, and all the days they had spent together—now they were being split apart? Frank didn't trust himself not to collapse into tears, so he gave Judy a quick tousle of the ears and told her to go on without him. He handed the leash to the government official.

"She stopped at the gangway," Frank remembered, "seemingly because she did not understand my command. Her questioning gaze and waggling tail suggested she expected me to summon her back. But as always on my command, she walked meekly toward the docks and jumped in the truck of the quarantine service."

Judy was a prisoner once more. And this time, she would have to bear it alone.

QUARANTINE

Judy's new home was called the Hackbridge Quarantine Kennels. They were in Surrey, about a twenty-minute train trip from London. In fact, you could hear the barking at the train station.

Judy was alone.

She couldn't leave.

But this was no prison camp. It was a beautiful home for dogs in a gorgeous wooded area. Judy might not have been happy without Frank, but surely she was content.

Upon arrival, she was thoroughly checked for disease and groomed in a way she hadn't been since the war started—maybe ever. Frank visited often, and the seventy-member staff at the kennels, once briefed on Judy's story, went out of their way to comfort her.

Hackbridge could handle six hundred animals, but there were far fewer when Judy was there. No two dogs could come in contact with each other, in order to protect the quarantine. They couldn't even exercise together—the complex required plenty of room for every dog to have its own space.

And so Judy got to explore the lush meadows and hedges of the Surrey countryside. She no longer had to hunt for her dinner. Instead, she was brought delicious food, including dog biscuits and even fresh vegetables. Many people in England didn't eat as well as the dogs of Hackbridge.

According to an essay in the *Tail-Wagger Magazine*, Judy would have been let out into her individual large paddock to run while her kennel was cleaned just after 8 a.m. The exercise period lasted half an hour. At 11 a.m. she would have been fed her main meal of the day, "a sight for canine eyes," according to the essay, dog food either dry or "covered with delicious meat gravy." The afternoon brought more runs, along with a nap and whatever visitors turned up to give Judy's ears a scruffing. Then a smaller snack of biscuits, one last trip outside, and lights-out at 7 p.m.

All in all, a pretty darn good life.

But it wasn't easy. Judy was an independent dog. She had showed that as a puppy, when she tunneled out of her Shanghai kennel. Even though the prison camps had been terrible, she had gotten to roam free in the jungle, looking for food and hiding from the guards. Living on a set schedule wasn't her style.

Frank had to pay for the cost of the boarding, which was about twelve pounds, or nearly fifty US dollars (over six hundred dollars in today's money). He didn't have much money, so to help him out, the Tail-Waggers Club put a notice in the December 1945 issue of its magazine, announcing that the organization was "opening a small fund to defray the cost of Judy's stay in quarantine. Should there be any surplus it will be paid to Judy's owner as a help toward her future maintenance."

Plenty of readers answered the call for help. The next issue of the club's "Official Organ" detailed the contributions: over thirty-five pounds in the end, far more than required.

That was the good news. Upon returning home, Frank had also received some bad news.

DAVID

As soon as Frank had handed Judy over to the quarantine official, he boarded a train from Liverpool bound for the RAF base at Cosford, about ninety minutes south in England's Midlands, in Shropshire. Cosford was the site of Personnel Reception Centre (PRC) #106. This was where all RAF POWs returning to England made their first stop. Thousands of prisoners had been held in the European theater, and England welcomed them back easily enough. But until the war ended, the number of POWs held by the Japanese was unknown. It turned out to be far larger than expected. So Cosford was kept open and working well into 1945.

This was in keeping with the entire Pacific war. While every detail of the war against the Germans was well known to the English populace, the suffering in the Pacific was far more a case of "out of sight, out of mind." The enormity of the terror faced by the POWs at the hands of the Japanese was only just being understood.

"The functional purpose of the unit is to receive, kit, medically examine and attend to the documentation of ex prisoner of war personnel" is how the British War Ministry described what the PRC was supposed to do. "After this procedure the ex prisoners of war proceed on 42 days leave, after which they return for a full medical board at the PRC."

The logs kept at Cosford report that two trainloads of former prisoners arrived on October 29, a group of 340 at 1:50 and another of 341 at 3:10. Frank was on one of these two trains. He was interviewed, "kitted" out with fresh RAF uniform gear, given back pay, including combat and special service pay, and looked over by the doctors. Frank's condition was improved enough after his weeks at sea to allow him to pass through the basic testing and debriefing and be released. He was free to go back to Portsmouth and his family for six weeks of leave, beginning as October turned to November.

Frank returned to his hometown, which was a far different place from the bustling port of his youth. The city had been thoroughly wrecked by bombs from Nazi air raids, most of the damage done during three major attacks from August 1940 to March 1941. Frank's family home at 38 Holland Road had been bracketed by explosions during the Fire Blitz of January 10 and 11, 1941, although it appears the house miraculously suffered little damage. But that was the rare tale of good fortune. Approximately 930 people were killed by the bombings, with 1,216 more wounded. This was tragic, though other parts of England had suffered even worse casualties. The city itself had been thoroughly wrecked, too. "Our principle shopping centres have been almost obliterated," wrote the *Portsmouth Evening News* in 1941. "There is not a part of the city which does not show hideous scars, in some places completely devastated areas." Thirty churches were leveled, as were eight schools and four cinemas. The city's well-known George Hotel was demolished, as was the tallest building, the Central Hotel.

All that was bad enough. But Frank got even worse news upon returning to his family. On June 6, 1944, his older brother, David, a private in the Royal Army, had been killed during the D-Day invasion of Europe (see sidebar). It wasn't until nearly a year and a half had passed that Frank heard about this untimely death. Frank was a youngster when he lost his father—now his big brother was also gone. He never really talked about his sadness. But it no doubt was a savage blow. And it came on top of Judy's being separated from his side.

D-DAY

Germany held on to all the countries it had invaded and conquered until the summer of 1944, when the Allies were ready to try to take them back. The United States and Great Britain staged a massive invasion across the English Channel, known as D-Day, on June 6, 1944. This was a very important moment in both World War Two and world history.

D-Day is a military phrase used to mean the chosen date of any large activity, like this invasion, which was so big and crucial that it has become the defining D-Day. The Allies gathered a gigantic army in England and took a huge fleet of ships across the body of water separating England from France, the English Channel. It was the single biggest invasion of the war, with roughly 150,000 men and nearly 7,000 vessels, from big destroyers to small craft that carried soldiers to the beaches.

The crossing of the Channel by the gigantic force was tricky, because it is a very rainy and windy area. The weather and tides were not ideal, but the decision was made to go ahead. The wind in particular caused a lot of trouble, blowing parachuting troops off course and even forcing boats away from their target areas. These were the beaches of the French region called Normandy. The beaches were given code names: Utah, Omaha, Gold, Juno, and Sword.

On the beaches, the German defenders were waiting. More than 4,000 Allied soldiers were killed on the sand, including

Frank's brother, and 10,000 more were wounded. It was a hard fight, but eventually, the Allied forces got ashore and secured the beach area.

From there, the Allied armies swept across France, Belgium, the Netherlands, and other countries, freeing them from the Nazis one by one. At last, the Allies crossed into Germany and forced its surrender, ending World War Two in Europe. The Japanese fought on for a few more months before they also gave in, and the war was finally over.

At some point, Frank, like all British POWs, would have been handed a letter from King George VI, welcoming him home.

The Queen and I bid you a very warm welcome home.

Through all the great trials and sufferings which you have undergone at the hands of the Japanese, you and your comrades have been constantly in our thoughts. We know from the accounts we have already received how heavy these sufferings have been. We also know that these have been endured by you with the highest courage.

We mourn with you the deaths of so many of your gallant comrades.

*With all our hearts, we hope that your return
from captivity will bring you and your families a full
measure of happiness, which you may long enjoy
together.*

Frank's leave in Portsmouth ended in mid-December, when he had to return to the air base at Cosford for a full medical evaluation. There is no record of any further treatment ordered for him. This means Frank apparently met the standards set by the staff for a return to duty. That wasn't the case for many of his fellow ex-POWs. A situation report from Cosford points out the difficulty many had in leaving the Japanese camps behind. "Medical board action in respect of Far East POWs proved much more lengthy and complicated than was the case with [POWs held in Europe], owing to the effect of malaria, dysentery, eye trouble and worms, and to the complete disregard which had been displayed by the Japanese in respect of all medical condition."

The malaria was really stubborn. Fred Freeman, a Pakan Baroe POW, was a good example. He returned to his prewar home in Brighton, on the southern coast of England, but the malaria attacks continued, to the point where he couldn't hold a job. He was forced to apply for a medical pension as a result. "The headaches persist," he wrote in his application. "In fact I had one all last night and this morning. Several times my employers have counted a day of illness as a day off to avoid losing cash."

It seemed the men could leave the prison camps, but the camps wouldn't leave them.

RECOVERY

At the start of 1946, Judy was getting used to her quarantine. Meanwhile, Frank was off to a new post.

It was a POW rehabilitation center (or "refresher," as the RAF called it) in Sunninghill Park, an estate outside London. It was a place for the POWs to really readapt to life back in England. Many had been away for years—some had served overseas long before the war began in 1939.

For three weeks the men were reminded how a country at peace worked. They were given lectures on civilian life. They were introduced to businessmen and government workers. They were told all about the war that had just finished—remember, Frank and the other POWs had been completely cut off from what was happening both at home and around the globe.

"Much time should be available for recreation and sports and games and gardening, music, amateur dramatics, farming, etc.," read an official Air Ministry report on these rehabilitation centers. There were visits by local orchestras, films shown in the station movie theater, a "liberal supply of bicycles for officers and airmen," and plenty of "citrus fruit available," as many returned POWs were lacking in vitamin C.

Rouse Voisey, who had been in a camp near Frank and Judy at Pakan Baroe, was there, too. Frank struck him as a gentle sort, "a nice, quiet chap, quite average, really." For Rouse, the rehab center did the trick. He found a job in the local government near Norwich, where he'd grown up, and spent thirty-two years as a civil servant.

Frank's thinking on returning home isn't exactly known. He didn't give any interviews about this time. In later years, he didn't talk much about what had happened to him. That wasn't unusual for POWs. Rouse gave one reason why. "The government told us not to talk about our experiences," he said, sixty-eight years later. "We just had to get on with it. No one wanted to make a fuss over us." It seems strange today that a government would hush up, rather than celebrate, the incredible bravery and endurance these POWs displayed, but it was a different time.

"Who knows why politicians do anything?" Rouse said with a chuckle.

There were other reasons for Frank to stay quiet. Some POWs heard about the horrors others had faced in the war and didn't want to start comparing their suffering. John Williams, another RAF man, who had been on Pompong Island with Frank, wrote about this in his memoir. "At the time, it did not seem appropriate to write in more graphic prose about some of the horrors and barbarities which we had witnessed or experienced, especially having regard to the much worse happenings that had occurred at Belsen and other Nazi concentration camps."

The British military anticipated this to some degree. "Among the symptoms to be expected," read a report prepared for the Cosford doctors, included "a sense of strangeness, shyness and reticence, a dislike of crowds, lack of concentration, mind changing, and a strong resentment against petty restrictions."

Frank likely displayed all of these in some form or another.

Think about his experience for a minute. His war had been humiliating. His country's forces had been booted off Singapore by the Japanese in record time. He ran away but was captured with ease. He was beaten up regularly. He had terrible diseases that put him flat on his back, helpless. For Frank, only one good thing had come out of the war—Judy. So that was pretty much the only thing he liked to talk about. It makes perfect sense, when you think about it.

Rouse Voisey remembered the love Frank had for Judy— the lanky radarman from Portsmouth talked of little save his best friend. "He was peddling pictures of Judy to us at the rehabilitation center," Rouse recalled. "They had information about her service and her adventures on the back. Somehow, Frank had gotten Judy's paw prints on there too. I bought a couple for a pound or two each, quite a small amount. The money was for charity. Frank was raising funds to give to [the People's Dispensary for Sick Animals, or PDSA]."

Upon leaving the rehab facility, Frank was assigned to a new RAF base—even though he had been through so much, he was still an airman on active duty. This was another reason why he was discouraged from saying anything about his days as a POW. Servicemen and servicewomen are supposed to act, not talk. Frank was assigned to the Number 4 Mobile Radar Unit at the RAF base in West Kirby, near Liverpool.

Then it was time to be reunited with Judy.

It had been a long six months for man and dog, but Judy was freed into Frank's care on April 29, 1946. Frank arrived

"Gunboat Judy" bids a fond farewell to one of her handlers upon her release from mandatory six-month quarantine after her arrival in England.

looking dapper in his Royal Air Force uniform. Judy was sleek and well groomed, having had a special long bubble bath that morning. Their meeting was joyous—"She was all legs and tongue," Frank remembered.

There was a ceremony to celebrate Judy's release, well attended by press photographers. The chairman of the British Kennel Club, Arthur Croxton Smith, presented Judy with a "For Valour" Medal of the Club and handed Frank the check to help him pay the kennel costs. This was the promised surplus from the fund-raising efforts of the Tail-Waggers Club. The club's magazine noted that "Mr. Williams requests to us to convey his thanks to all the people concerned who have contributed so generously toward Judy's Quarantine expenses." A representative of Spratt's Patent Limited, a dog food maker, also slipped a new collar onto the pointer's neck, to go with her existing one, which still sported her POW number, 81-A. The new collar was inscribed PRESENTED TO JUDY, EX-JAP-P.O.W., BY SPRATT'S.

Then Frank and Judy left for London, to go be heroes.

Getty Images

Frank grooms Judy before one of her many public appearances.

HEROES

During her six months of quarantine, the story of Judy's incredible journey and survival had made her a national heroine. The papers were filled with tales of her amazing adventures and her incredible defiance of the Japanese. The press called her Gunboat Judy and the Precious Pointer. On May 3, 1946, there was a ceremony honoring her service in west London's Cadogan Square, a fancy, wealthy neighborhood. It was staged by the PDSA, for which Frank was already raising money. The PDSA was (and still is) a veterinary charity founded in 1917 by Maria Dickin. It works with animals who belong to poor and suffering people.

In 1943, with animals contributing to the war effort across all branches of the service, Maria Dickin had established the Dickin Medal, an animal version of the Victoria Cross, the highest honor in the realm. Thirty-five animals had won the award, including eleven dogs and plenty of messenger pigeons, including three named Winkie, White Vision, and Tyke (aka George). The birds were used to carry important instructions across battlefields or behind enemy lines, from one unit to another. In these cases, the pigeons were given medals for "delivering a message under exceptionally difficult conditions and so contributing to the rescue of an Air Crew."

Now it was Judy's turn.

The seventy-six-year-old Dickin, herself much honored by the king, was there to watch. Major Roderick Mackenzie, also known as the Fourth Earl of Cromartie, also known as Viscount Tarbat (the English love to give special names to the upper-crust nobility), was the chairman of the Returned British POW Association. He stepped forward to give Judy her Dickin Medal. The pointer sat casually as the medal was pinned to her collar.

Frank beamed with pride.

Getty Images

Judy is awarded the Dickin Medal in a ceremony in May 1946. Frank is on the right; Major Roderick Mackenzie, chairman of the Returned British POW Association, is on the left.

243

The citation that came with the medal read:

**FOR MAGNIFICENT COURAGE AND ENDURANCE IN
JAPANESE PRISON CAMPS THUS HELPING TO
MAINTAIN MORALE AMONG HER FELLOW PRISONERS
AND FOR SAVING MANY LIVES BY HER
INTELLIGENCE AND WATCHFULNESS.**

At the same ceremony, Frank also was given an award. It was the PDSA's White Cross of St. Giles, the highest award given to humans by the group. He got it for his

Image Works

Judy poses with other winners of the Dickin Medal.

special devotion to Judy. Major Mackenzie pinned it to his tunic, and man and dog smiled for the many photographers there to mark the moment.

Honor followed honor during the next several weeks. It was a whirlwind. Britain was at long last truly celebrating the victory in World War Two. Judy was treated as a hero, like the generals and servicemembers who had helped defeat the Third Reich. The Tail-Waggers Club, adding to its previous gift, gave Frank a large (undisclosed) sum to ensure that Judy never wanted for food or shelter again. Judy was given a party at the Returned British POW Association in London, where she was enrolled by Major Mackenzie as an official member—needless to say, the only dog in the rolls.

On June 8, 1946, came the Victory Day celebrations, which included parades, fireworks, water cannons, orchestras providing music for dancing across London, and an appearance by the king. "This is your day—enjoy it," the *London Daily Mirror* told the people of Britain. Frank and Judy were chosen to be part of a special episode of the popular BBC radio program *In Town Tonight*, along with soldiers and sailors and airmen from every place the war was fought. The host, Roy Rich, asked Judy to say something to the listeners at home.

Right on cue, Judy barked loudly into the microphone.

"This happy barking echoed in a lot of houses all over

the world," said Frank, who was right alongside Judy for all the fun. "Even in Singapore people could hear this dog 'talking.'" Later on, the duo appeared on BBC television, on the show *Picture Page*, which aired in the afternoon and evening (Judy barked happily on both programs, while legendary songwriter Irving Berlin looked on).

Another huge extravaganza Judy attended was a show at London's fabled Wembley Stadium. It was called "Stars of Blitz and Battlefront." Three other dogs that had been

Judy and Frank appear on the BBC television show Picture Page, *hosted by Wynford Vaughan-Thomas, on September 9, 1946.*

heroes during the war appeared alongside Judy to receive the love and warmth of eighty-two thousand spectators in the stadium (see sidebar).

One of the other dogs was named Rob, "a sturdy collie crossbreed," in Frank's description. Rob was trained to be a paratrooper, and jumped along with the elite British Special Air Service commandos behind enemy lines on several missions. Judy and Rob had met frequently on the "hero dog" circuit and had become friendly. They had bonded, like any good action-movie buddies, over a brawl. At a different appearance, Judy and Rob were waiting in the wings to go onstage when a quartet of tall brown Borzois strutted past. Borzois are Russian wolfhounds, closely related to greyhounds, and like that speedy breed, Borzois are quite high-strung.

When Borzoi met pointer backstage, one of the Russian dogs leapt at Judy and bit her. "At that instance," recalled Frank, "the arena changed into a battlefield of fighting dogs." Rob jumped in to defend Judy's honor, while all four Borzois attacked together. The two-against-four fight whirled behind the curtain while the show went on in front of it. Judy and Rob stood their ground as "brown hair flakes flew in all directions," Frank remembered. When at last the dogs were separated, the Borzois had lost the brawl. Their performance had to be canceled.

Another great escape by Judy!

WAR DOGS

Dogs have fought alongside man in combat since at least the seventh century BCE. During World War Two, dogs helped fight in a variety of ways. They sniffed out enemy ambushes, detected mines, guarded sensitive areas, and hunted for wounded men and women. There was even a battalion of British dogs that dropped from the air as paratroopers behind the front lines.

Rip was a mongrel terrier who became famous for rescuing Brits trapped by bomb damage. The plucky little dog found more than a hundred survivors buried in the rubble, earning him the Dickin Medal, the top commendation an animal can receive (Judy also won the Dickin upon liberation).

Chips, a mixed breed (a little Husky, some collie, and some German shepherd), was part of the first War Dog Detachment to be sent overseas with American troops. It was in Sicily in 1943 when Chips spotted an enemy position, broke away from his handler, and attacked the machine-gun crew inside. He seized one man and forced the entire four-man crew to surrender. In recognition of his service, Chips was awarded several medals, including the Silver Star and the Purple Heart.

But after the war, the Pentagon decided that awarding citations to dogs was "contrary to Army policy" and stripped Chips of his medals. This is the going explanation as to why Chips reacted to meeting General Dwight D. Eisenhower by biting him.

Other dogs paid the ultimate price for their service. Wolf, US Army War Dog T121, was a Doberman, and a brave one. He was leading an infantry patrol in the mountains of northern Luzon in the Philippines when the scent of an enemy patrol wafted past his powerful nose. His warning allowed the American patrol to take favorable positions on a hillside. In the ensuing fire fight, Wolf suffered shrapnel wounds but stoically stayed quiet, not allowing the Japanese to pinpoint where the soldiers were. Wolf then led the withdrawal, sniffing out ambushes three times. At last, the US soldiers made it to headquarters, where Wolf was rushed into emergency surgery. Alas, his wounds were too severe. Wolf died on the operating table.

Then there was Gander, a massive Newfoundland from eastern Canada. He went with his Royal Canadian Rifles regiment to try to prevent the Japanese from taking Hong Kong in late 1941. To flush out the Canadian troops, the Japanese infantry tossed many grenades at them. A "pineapple" landed in the center of a group of Canadians. Suddenly a streak of black fur dashed in and seized the sizzling grenade. It was Gander! The dog ran off, getting about twenty yards from the men before the grenade exploded. It took more than fifty years, but Gander's sacrifice was at last recognized in 1996, when he, too, was awarded the Dickin Medal.

Judy became a regular at fund-raising drives for all manner of causes. She marched in a seemingly endless parade that stretched from the far north of Scotland to the shores of Brighton on England's southern tip. She took in dog shows, such as the large one in Bath that attracted "311 entrants and some 1,500 people," according to the *Bath Chronicle*, including the mayor of Bath. "The appearance of Judy, the 11-years-old English pointer...was the signal for crowds of spectators to leave the rings and go to the foot of the stage, where L.A.C. Williams [that's Frank], her owner, introduced Judy to her admirers." Indeed, Frank was by her side for every appearance, and Judy never strayed far from him, even as the masses pressed in to stroke or get a glimpse of the heroic dog.

Judy got to meet many stars of stage and screen along the way, who were all unfailingly charmed by her. The popular English actor and future Oscar winner David Niven reportedly called her the "loveliest [dog] he had ever clapped eyes on." Frank would surely agree, as would the many other servicemen who had befriended and fallen hard for Judy in Asia.

Judy's most valuable days were spent in children's hospitals and in the living rooms of other returned prisoners, or with the families of those who had not come home. She was always a comfort to the sick kids or the sorrowful relatives, and she made these visits as an official member of the Royal Air Force. Even though she had started off in the Royal Navy, Frank had arranged for Judy to become the mascot of his air force base, so Judy was now an airdog. She wore a coat with an embroidered RAF crest to match Frank's uniform. Frank made sure that Judy also wore her other campaign ribbons honoring her service on these visits.

Because Judy was doing well after the war had ended, she was a bright example for the many POWs who struggled to adapt to life back in England. During the war, she had buoyed many men in the jungle by simply enduring. In peacetime, she set an ideal once more.

There was one other task Frank and Judy performed,

this one far more difficult. Countless family members of POWs had been told only that the soldier or sailor or flier they loved dearly was missing or deceased. They had no other information. Many clung to hopes that their loved ones were still alive.

Some of them reached out to the suddenly famous pointer, sending her letters via the RAF or the War Ministry or sometimes simply to "Judy," with no address. Many letters managed to find their way to Frank. All that these people wanted was more information about the husband or son or brother or father who had never come home from the war.

"Judy and I travelled throughout England to inform the mourning family that their family member was not rotting in the Sumatran jungle," said Frank. "It was not an easy exercise, explaining to someone the inhumane circumstances wherein a mate had died."

Some of the deceased hadn't actually been held prisoner in an area near Frank and Judy's camps, but that really wasn't the point. Frank and Judy *had* survived and had come home. Often, the sad families merely wanted to spend some time with this unlikely pair who had beaten the odds. As Frank noted, "The presence of Judy seemed in a way to soften the essence of these sad times and brought some comfort with many families that had lived for months or years in uncertainty about the facts."

It was a busy time for Frank and Judy, but eventually, things started to slow down. On July 22, 1946, Frank and Judy left the air force. The exit ceremony took place at the RAF Technical Training Command Centre, on the banks of the River Dee near Liverpool. Judy wore her medals and ribbons on her collar and stood at attention. The proceedings took a few minutes, and then the two best friends walked out past the gate.

They were now civilians. Their military careers were over.

Frank took Judy back home to Portsmouth, the southern naval town of his youth, where so many ships had been launched (including Judy's former homes, the *Gnat* and the *Grasshopper*). There, he started to wonder what he was going to do with the rest of his life.

Whatever it was, Judy would be part of it, that much he was sure of. And after all they'd been through, that was all that mattered.

PORTSMOUTH

Life in Portsmouth was quiet and dull, which for a time suited Frank Williams and his dog just fine.

It isn't exactly known whether they moved back to his family home at 38 Holland Road. Voting records indicate that while Frank's mother, Agnes, as well as his sisters Barbara and Jean Williams, cast ballots from that address in 1947, Frank did not. A Frank Williams did vote from an address in the northern part of the city, however. It seems likely Frank and Judy moved there. After all he had been through, surely Frank wanted a place of his own for him and his dog. His family home was crowded and no doubt carried painful memories of his fallen older brother, David.

Frank talked about bringing Judy to his local pub, the Stamshaw Hotel, which was also in the northern part of town. Judy loved being the center of attention and the main topic of conversation at the pub, and she was often recognized around town, too. "Look, there goes the famous war dog," people would say.

But simple Portsmouth existence had some drawbacks, too. After the epic struggle for life that both man and dog had lived through the past few years, it was hard to summon up the energy to work a normal job. Frank's family members mentioned this on a tribute website in 2003. "England's societal niceties seemed superficial and somewhat ridiculous to him after his experiences in the camps," they wrote. This was a typical feeling among returned POWs.

In addition, there were other factors in Frank's growing discontent. Lizzie Oliver, a POW historian whose grandfather was held at Pakan Baroe, said that during that time "families either went overboard mollycoddling the returned men, or they went the other way and it was never spoken of again. Neither method really worked out well." POW John Hedley said his family "had the perception that we had such a rough time of it that we wouldn't be normal.

And they treated us as such—we were mollycoddled. And I had a hard time handling that. It's one of the reasons why after just under six months I was back in my old job in Malaya...to be understood, if you like, to feel normal" (see sidebar).

Frank surely didn't like the idea of being cared for too much, so he almost never talked of his experiences in the camps. He was always happy to show off Judy and brag about her courage, though.

Meanwhile, many returning prisoners found the United Kingdom "quite grim and miserable," in Lizzie Oliver's words, after a war spent in the tropics. Even though they had been held as prisoners and had endured the worst possible conditions, many POWs missed the blue skies, green rain forests, and turquoise seas of the Pacific. "By contrast," said Oliver, "the bleak landscape of England in winter led many of them to wonder, 'Is this all there is?'" It didn't help that the winter of 1946–47 was extremely cold and snowy, requiring emergency power cuts across the country for weeks. Factories shut down everywhere, leaving millions of people without work. The country lived by candlelight for much of January and February 1947.

Portsmouth itself was very slow to rebuild after the war. The city was still in piles of rubble well into the

1950s, years after the Germans had bombed it to bits. There were shortages of material and manpower, and the national economy was bad. In fact, the first shop on Portsmouth's Commercial Road didn't reopen until 1952. "For years after the war you were putting in reports that read, 'It was on the bomb site on such-and-such a road,'" recalled a frustrated local policeman of the years after the war. In other words, there were no other landmarks, just bomb craters.

The historic homes that had lent character to Portsmouth were gone. In their place came bland, cookie-cutter "council flats," government houses that were extremely ugly, if cheap.

Frank was holding everything inside. He was living in a cold, bombed-out shell of a town. Great Britain was no longer so great. The jobs he held were work, not a career.

What we do know for sure is that life in England got very boring very quickly. Frank had always been looking for escapes, even as a kid. He'd gone to sea at age sixteen! Then he'd joined the service and gone to war. Hanging around town just wasn't in his nature. Judy, of course, was always up for a new adventure.

So when an opportunity to travel far from home came up, Frank and Judy jumped at it.

PTSD

Post-traumatic stress disorder (PTSD) is a syndrome that often strikes POWs, soldiers, and others who live through war. After violent, troubling experiences, it becomes very difficult to live a "normal" life. It isn't known for sure whether Frank suffered from this particular kind of postwar mental pain. But it would have been hard for him to merely shrug off the awfulness of his war experience. Unfortunately, PTSD and other conditions like it were not really understood at that time. Frank could have suffered from it and not even realized what was wrong.

Few POWs had the capacity to deal with the suffering and imprisonment the way Rouse Voisey did—by essentially ignoring his time in the camps completely. "Perhaps nature has wiped it from my mind," he has said recently, "but I blanked out a lot of the worst of it. Sure, I have nightmares on and off, but I'm mostly okay with what happened to me. I think I actually learned how to do that in the camps—how to shut things out. There it was a necessity, you couldn't last any other way."

And what of Frank's dog? Judy was outwardly fat and happy, up to her heaviest-ever weight of sixty-one pounds. Her once solidly brown snout was turning white with age, but otherwise she appeared to be a healthy, loving dog.

But it is possible that she, too, was having trouble dealing with the aftermath of the horror she survived. Human PTSD wasn't understood after World War Two. The canine version was utterly impossible for anyone to comprehend.

Recent science has confirmed that dogs can and do suffer from a form of PTSD. Around seven hundred dogs have seen action in the recent wars in Iraq and Afghanistan, and some researchers estimate that between 5 and 10 percent of these animals have suffered traumatic stress disorder from it.

The syndrome can also develop in household pets that have never been anywhere near a war. Dogs that get mistreated by humans, as Judy had been, or live with no shelter or love can suffer as well. Many animal lovers make a point of adopting or caring for dogs that have once been abused, giving their pets a brighter future.

AFRICA

It was called the Groundnut Scheme.

Britain was facing food shortages after the war. The government decided on a plan of action. There were areas of Africa that belonged to the British Empire— one of these countries was called Tanganyika (it is now Tanzania).

The idea was to plant massive, sweeping crops there, of peanuts and other nuts that grow on the ground (most nuts grow on trees). This would be a cheap way to get some nutrition to the British people.

The program needed people to oversee the planting, growing, and harvesting of the nuts. Frank applied for a position and was hired by the Overseas Food Corporation, which was the chief organizing body in charge of the Groundnut Scheme.

Peanuts require a great deal of water to grow properly. Unfortunately, the areas chosen to plant them were drought-stricken. The Groundnut Scheme collapsed after several years of failure and ultimately became a symbol of England's postwar decline. By 1960, Ian Fleming, in his James Bond story "Quantum of Solace," would have a character refer to a tragic figure who "after a lifetime of service gets shunted off into the groundnuts scheme."

But Frank didn't see it that way. He wanted to go to Africa. There was just one problem.

They didn't want Judy to come along.

It looked like the Groundnut Scheme would do what the Japanese, the ocean, and the jungle had failed to do— separate Frank from his dog. Try as he might, he couldn't get permission for Judy to come with him. It was far away, after all, and the job would keep Frank very busy. The *Evening Standard* of March 20, 1948, reported on the crisis, noting that "man and dog have not been parted for six years," except during the quarantine, and that "young Frank Williams, who should be a happy man today... fears he will never see [Judy] again."

Frank asked if the PDSA might be able to help. Some-one there called the mastermind behind the plan, Lord Leverhulme, whose business firm Lever Brothers was providing the money for the project. Once the big cheese heard that the famous Judy wasn't to be allowed to partici-pate in his brainchild, he threw a fit—and all resistance to Judy's travel melted away.

No one could keep Frank and Judy apart.

Judy took her first airplane flights traveling from En-gland to Africa. She handled herself just fine, except for one incident. The plane landed in Egypt to refuel. A customs offi-cial came aboard with a spray gun loaded with germ killer. Judy was apparently dead asleep in the aisle. But when she sensed a man with a gun coming near, she snapped awake and became the old Judy. Baring her teeth and snarling, she chased the shocked official off the plane, across the tarmac, and all the way to the door of the airport building. He man-aged to slam and lock the door just ahead of the mad dog.

Judy strolled back onto the plane, "grinning like the Cheshire Cat," according to Frank. He felt it was all a show, just something to chase away the boredom. Judy always did have a sense of the moment.

On the ground in Tanganyika, Frank was sent to the city of Kongwa for training. He was to be responsible for a

Two best friends pose for a portrait taken in 1948, just before they left for Africa.

large area of planting centered in the Nachingwea District in the southeast part of the nation.

It was rough terrain, so Judy and Frank were constantly driving in a Land Rover, bouncing all over the countryside. Frank was routinely spending hours each day traveling between growing sites and the villages in between. The car was designed to hold up to a dozen passengers, and it was usually crammed, but room was always made for Judy.

It was easy to readapt to life in the bush. Snakes, baboons, and elephants made more sense to Judy than did taxicabs, trolleys, and manicured lawns. "She was at her best when traveling through unsoiled nature," Frank recalled. "She was able to live her hunting instincts by chasing a diversity of wild animals." Incredibly enough, her first action upon seeing a herd of elephants trumpeting through the savanna was to point them out with classic pointer form. She had never done it right before, but somehow her natural instinct was finally unleashed.

If only the men from the *Gnat* could have seen her! Her paw perfectly raised, her head and tail straight as a ruler in a direct line toward the pachyderms.

"Stop showing off, Judy, I see them," Frank muttered.

Judy was very careful around the enormous creatures in Africa. But she wasn't scared of them, a fact she proved late one night outside Frank's hut. Frank's domestic helper, Abdul, had taken the bathtub outside so it could be emptied in the morning. At around 2 a.m., man and dog heard what sounded like a giant vacuum cleaner operating just outside. Judy raced out the door and started barking furiously. Frank looked and saw a large bull elephant noisily sucking the water in the tub down his trunk, the full moon perfectly illuminating the scene.

Judy was racing back and forth, barking and leaping at the elephant's trunk, then his tail, as though unable to decide where she wanted to concentrate her fire. The elephant, tired of the irritating animal at his feet, lumbered away without any further incident. That wasn't victory enough for the pointer, however. She seized the tub in her teeth and hauled it back inside the hut. With a final deep bark of warning back out into the night, she lay down, her job finished for the evening.

Judy had less luck chasing the baboons that always seemed to be around. These baboons came at her in waves, entire families up for a game of tag Judy could never win. Anytime she tried to grab one, they ran up a tree and disappeared. A group of the animals would jump all about her, turning Judy this way and that. It was very frustrating. Judy played along for a while, but when the monkeys began hurling corncobs and sticks at her, she gave up and ceased playing with them.

Stupid monkeys.

Frank took Judy with him once on a flight to the capital city of Tanganyika, Dar Es Salaam. He was worried about her—Judy would be forced to fly in a small kennel for the first time, unlike on the flights to Africa, where she could roam the aisles at will. As it turned out, Judy was perfectly silent for the length of the flight. Frank discovered why when he went to retrieve her. The kennel had a hole cut at the top so she could stick her head out, and someone had left a slab of fresh beef within chewing distance.

Judy had eaten almost the whole thing.

From Shanghai to Sumatra, Judy had learned the hard way that she shouldn't ever pass up a meal. The huge lunch left a visible bulge in her belly, making her resemble an anaconda after it had devoured a goat. Frank picked her up and raced off the plane and into his Jeep before the owner of the meat could discover that it had disappeared down Judy's gullet. Frank tried to be angry with her, but he could hardly stop laughing.

Judy took so well to Africa that she even became a mother once again.

The father remained anonymous, just as at Gloegoer. But this time, there were plenty of other dogs around, so the pregnancy wasn't a total mystery. One fine day in 1949, Judy gave birth for the third time. Seven pups were born.

She now had given birth to twenty-six pups, born across eleven years, spanning three countries on two continents. She became a mother aboard a warship, in a prison camp, and while farming in the African bush.

Hopefully, her newborn pups would get to live a far more peaceful and happy life than Judy did.

JUDY DISAPPEARS

On January 26, 1950, Frank loaded Judy into his Land Rover. He drove about twelve miles from his home in the bush. The Groundnut Scheme now included some mining operations, and Frank was to inspect one of the mines. Judy hung around the area for a little while, but she soon "went hunting on her own," according to Frank.

Judy was fourteen years old. Her brown-and-white coat was getting increasingly gray. Her age also showed in her face and when she ran. She wasn't nearly as quick and energetic as she used to be.

An explorer at heart, she remained happiest when she

ranged far and wide in the wild. She also always returned to meet Frank when it was time to go home.

But on this day, she didn't answer his whistle. She was nowhere to be found, not having "returned from her safari," as Frank put it. He whistled again and again, but no pointer came streaking in from the bush.

"It was about four o'clock in the afternoon when I went looking for her together with some of the remaining workers in the mining area," Frank remembered. "Unfortunately, without any result. At dusk we had to stop our efforts in finding her. We made as much publicity about Judy's disappearance as possible and offered a reward for anyone that could find her."

A careful search turned up her tracks. There was reason for alarm, though—there were also leopard tracks nearby. There was no sign of either animal in the flesh. Frank combed the countryside with Abdul but found nothing. He offered villagers rewards if they came across her. The days passed, and everyone gave up hope, except Frank.

Finally, a group of tribesmen showed up at his door. The men surrounded Abdul and talked and pointed wildly. Excited, Abdul got the message.

"They've seen Judy!" he cried.

She had been spotted near the village of Chumbawalla, a few hours away. The sun was already setting, and soon night would drop quickly, as it always did on the African plain. It made sense to wait until morning. But Frank was frantic. He set off straightaway.

He drove madly into the darkness, going far too fast for the unpaved roadways. He crossed roaring rivers, including one where the bridge had been washed away. Still he pushed on. At last, a short time before dawn, he arrived in the village.

Frank gave more than one account of what happened next. At one point he said he encountered the headman of the village, who took him to a low thatched hut. Inside was Judy, who was in bad shape. She got up, excited to see Frank, then collapsed with a whine.

Later, Frank told a slightly different story. He said that "after a conversation with the chief and the village eldest they agreed to organize a search party. This time with success, because Judy was grabbed the next day and held until I came to get her. She looked awful and was exhausted due to malnourishment."

Either way, Judy and Frank were together again.

Judy had been so at home in the deepest, darkest, most impenetrable jungles. She had always made it out okay. This time, though, she'd gotten lost and was badly shaken. Exactly why is a mystery. It's quite possible she was spooked by or perhaps chased by a leopard or some other large animal. Her usually perfect ability to navigate, keyed by her amazing nose, had been scrambled. At her advanced age, she was unable to bounce back easily. She was clearly in bad condition when she stumbled into the village and had resisted attempts to comfort her. Most likely, she was still trying to sniff out a familiar smell that would lead her back to Frank.

Frank spent hours bathing Judy, removing the numerous cattle ticks that had attached themselves to her coat. She was given a meal of chicken and milk to try to get some protein into her.

After devouring her dinner, Judy rolled over and slept for twelve hours straight. "After a couple of days, she seemed to be recovering perfectly," Frank said. Indeed, Judy regained some of her old bounce.

But on the evening of February 16, she awoke and began to cry. Frank stayed with her and tried to lull her back to sleep, but she would wake up and cry at least once an hour. She could scarcely walk and was clearly in terrible pain. In the morning, Frank carried her to the Nachingwea veterinary hospital. Judy was still crying in his arms. As he went into the hospital, Frank was worried sick. He couldn't reply when people said hello to him. He could barely control his voice when the chief surgeon of the hospital, a Dr. Jenkins, came to see him.

It turned out Judy's awful pain was coming from a cancerous tumor. "It was a race against time to get her up to strength as quickly as possible so that she could undergo the surgery to remove the tumor," Frank recalled.

Dr. Jenkins operated as soon as he dared. It seemed to work. The tumor was gone.

But soon a tetanus infection set in, and Judy was in even worse pain. She began shaking and shuddering with convulsions that racked her entire frame. She lost a lot of weight, looking more and more like the skeleton she had been in the prison camps. There wasn't much the hospital could do to ease her suffering.

Dr. Jenkins went to see Frank, who was trying to sleep on a small couch in the waiting room. But of course Frank couldn't rest easy, not while Judy was in agony. The doctor had been friendly with Frank and Judy since the day they arrived in Africa. Much as it pained him to say it, Judy's extraordinary life was in its final moments. Despite his sentiment, and Frank's, it was time to be firm.

"Let me end it, Frank," he said.

Frank could only nod and turn away.

Tears rolled down his cheeks.

Wordlessly, he followed Dr. Jenkins into the small room where Judy lay on a small bed, in terrible pain. Frank watched the vet prepare the needle.

Judy was put down via injection at five o'clock in the afternoon, local time, on February 17, 1950.

MEMORIAL

Judy was buried in her RAF jacket, in a grave close to Frank's hut in Africa.

She also wore her many awards, which included the Pacific Star campaign medal, the 1939–1945 Star, and the Defence Medal, awarded to all participants in the war. Stones were placed over the grave to keep the hyenas away.

Frank then began his last service for his great friend.

Day after day, hour after hour, he would venture out into the bush looking for white marble. No matter how many hours he worked during the day, he found time to hunt for the stone. He would cover wide areas without raising his gaze from the dirt, searching for that telltale gleam of white catching the sun. The marble came in large chunks, which Frank broke down into small bits, hammering away into the wee hours of the night.

He then mixed the marble with concrete and poured it over Judy's grave. He spent many more weeks shaping the marble slab. His goal was to make a monument for Judy that he thought equaled her love and extraordinary devotion. In his own words, it was to be a "worthy monument for an exceptionally brave dog who was an example of friendship, brave and courageous in all, even the most difficult, circumstances and who meant so much for so many when they lost courage."

When the slab was finished, he attached a metal plaque to its side. He had etched a tribute to Judy.

It read:

IN MEMORY OF
JUDY DM CANINE VC
BREED ENGLISH POINTER
BORN SHANGHAI FEBRUARY 1936
DIED FEBRUARY 1950
WOUNDED 14TH FEBRUARY 1942
BOMBED AND SUNK HMS GRASSHOPPER

LINGGA ARCHIPELAGO
FEBRUARY 14TH 1942
TORPEDOED SS VAN WAERWIJCK
MALACCA STRAIT JUNE 26 1943
JAPANESE PRISONER OF WAR MARCH
1942–AUGUST 1945
CHINA CEYLON JAVA ENGLAND
EGYPT BURMA
SINGAPORE MALAYA SUMATRA
EAST AFRICA
THEY ALSO SERVED
"A REMARKABLE CANINE…A GALLANT
OLD GIRL WHO WITH A WAGGING TAIL
GAVE MORE IN COMPANIONSHIP THAN
SHE EVER RECEIVED…AND WAS IN HER
SHORT LIFETIME AN INSPIRATION OF
COURAGE, HOPE AND A WILL TO LIVE,
TO MANY WHO WOULD HAVE GIVEN
UP IN THEIR TIME OF TRIAL HAD IT
NOT BEEN FOR HER EXAMPLE
AND FORTITUDE."

But such an extraordinary creature, and such an exceptional life, didn't simply end there. More than a half century after her death, Judy's bravery and service still inspired others.

It started when some men who had served with her on the gunboats in China and Singapore got together and compiled Judy's full story of adventure and endurance in a book published in England in 1973 called *The Judy Story*. Periodically after that, Judy was recognized in the United Kingdom in print and, most notably, by the Imperial War Museum (IWM) in London. In 2006, the IWM mounted a retrospective of animals who had served bravely in wartime, and Judy was front and center in the display.

Perhaps the most touching tribute to the wonderful pointer came on February 27, 1972. In naval towns across Britain, including Portsmouth, Judy's name was read aloud in remembrance of the dead, and church bells pealed in her honor. The London *Times*, in noting the event, called Judy "the shaggiest and saltiest seadog that ever howled in an ancient mariner's nightmare," making the friendly brown-and-white Judy sound more like a kraken than a mascot. The article also quoted one of Judy's old shipmates from the *Gnat*, a man named Bill Wilson, a medical attendant, who perhaps said it best: "It is right that she should be remembered for her magnificent valour at sea; she is an inspiration to all sailors."

Not just sailors—Judy was an inspiration to everyone who knew her and heard about her amazing life.

The memorial Frank created for Judy upon her death in Tanzania in 1950.

EPILOGUE

Shortly after burying Judy, Frank Williams almost died, too.

He was flying in a plane that crashed on the slopes of Mount Kilimanjaro, which borders Tanganyika and Kenya. But Frank had survived too much to perish now. He walked away from the crash uninjured and made it back to England in one piece.

By that point, Frank had much to live for. He had once again found a close companion—this time it was another person. An Englishwoman living in Africa had heard about a man who was searching far and wide for the proper memorial for his recently departed dog. The woman sought out the grieving man and grew close to him. Her name was Doris, and Frank married her upon returning to England.

The couple had three children, two boys and a girl. Each was born in a different country, for Frank never could stay put in England. He had visited Vancouver, a beautiful city in western Canada, while in the merchant navy. Many years later, he remembered how nice it was and decided to move his family there permanently.

He became an engineer, helping on construction projects all over the world. But his most important building was his family's home. He built it from scratch in the suburb of Burnaby. His kids called it Fort Williams.

Frank stayed an animal lover. In 2004, his daughter, Ann, wrote of her father's touch with nature. "He had a way with animals that I have not experienced with anyone else. They always understood him, and always adored him. If an animal was found hurt or suffering, they knew somehow to put their trust in him, and could relax at the sound of his voice, or his caring touch." Ann kept ponies as a girl, and they would invariably follow Frank around the field and crowd around him as he fixed up a fence. He once found a lost skunk and kept it as a pet, often taking it on long walks. "He would wake us up as kids in the middle of the night because he discovered something cool," Frank's son Alan told the *Vancouver Sun*, once to show the children a giant toad he had found in the backyard.

Of course, Frank's special relationship with Judy was one his family knew all about. "He didn't advertise it by any means," Alan told the *Burnaby Now* newspaper, "but he was happy to talk about it. If you got him going about it, he wouldn't stop. Probably the folks he worked with knew about it, but he didn't go out of his way to say, 'By the way, did you know I had a dog who was a heroine?'

"I think personally the bond he created saved his life," Alan continued. "I think she added an element to his life that gave him more reason to live. She took care of him, and he took care of her."

In 1992, at the age of seventy-three, Frank underwent minor surgery. While recovering in the hospital, he fell out of his bed. The fall left him confined to a wheelchair. It was a cruel blow after such an active life.

Frank hung on for roughly ten years after the fall. He died on February 16, 2003, one month after his eighty-fourth birthday. On display at Frank's funeral service at the Forest Lawn Chapel in Burnaby was a picture of Frank and Judy.

His second son, David, wrote on the memorial website devoted to Frank's memory this touching eulogy: "The only thing that helps me to overcome my grief is the knowledge that you are strolling leisurely along the warm sands of some heavenly beach...laughing at Judy, while she valiantly defends the shoreline from yet another impending wave."

Frank lived for fifty-three years after Judy died. He never again owned a dog.

TIMELINE

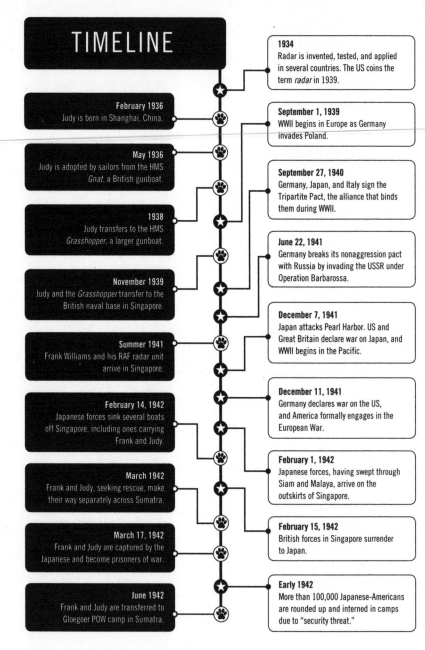

1934
Radar is invented, tested, and applied in several countries. The US coins the term *radar* in 1939.

February 1936
Judy is born in Shanghai, China.

September 1, 1939
WWII begins in Europe as Germany invades Poland.

May 1936
Judy is adopted by sailors from the HMS *Gnat*, a British gunboat.

September 27, 1940
Germany, Japan, and Italy sign the Tripartite Pact, the alliance that binds them during WWII.

1938
Judy transfers to the HMS *Grasshopper*, a larger gunboat.

June 22, 1941
Germany breaks its nonaggression pact with Russia by invading the USSR under Operation Barbarossa.

November 1939
Judy and the *Grasshopper* transfer to the British naval base in Singapore.

December 7, 1941
Japan attacks Pearl Harbor. US and Great Britain declare war on Japan, and WWII begins in the Pacific.

Summer 1941
Frank Williams and his RAF radar unit arrive in Singapore.

December 11, 1941
Germany declares war on the US, and America formally engages in the European War.

February 14, 1942
Japanese forces sink several boats off Singapore, including ones carrying Frank and Judy.

February 1, 1942
Japanese forces, having swept through Siam and Malaya, arrive on the outskirts of Singapore.

March 1942
Frank and Judy, seeking rescue, make their way separately across Sumatra.

February 15, 1942
British forces in Singapore surrender to Japan.

March 17, 1942
Frank and Judy are captured by the Japanese and become prisoners of war.

June 1942
Frank and Judy are transferred to Gloegoer POW camp in Sumatra.

Early 1942
More than 100,000 Japanese-Americans are rounded up and interned in camps due to "security threat."

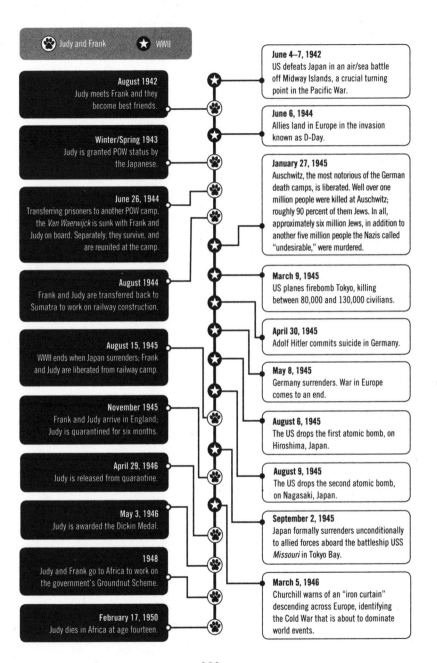

Judy and Frank · **WWII**

August 1942
Judy meets Frank and they become best friends.

Winter/Spring 1943
Judy is granted POW status by the Japanese.

June 26, 1944
Transferring prisoners to another POW camp, the *Van Waerwijck* is sunk with Frank and Judy on board. Separately, they survive, and are reunited at the camp.

August 1944
Frank and Judy are transferred back to Sumatra to work on railway construction.

August 15, 1945
WWII ends when Japan surrenders; Frank and Judy are liberated from railway camp.

November 1945
Frank and Judy arrive in England; Judy is quarantined for six months.

April 29, 1946
Judy is released from quarantine.

May 3, 1946
Judy is awarded the Dickin Medal.

1948
Judy and Frank go to Africa to work on the government's Groundnut Scheme.

February 17, 1950
Judy dies in Africa at age fourteen.

June 4–7, 1942
US defeats Japan in an air/sea battle off Midway Islands, a crucial turning point in the Pacific War.

June 6, 1944
Allies land in Europe in the invasion known as D-Day.

January 27, 1945
Auschwitz, the most notorious of the German death camps, is liberated. Well over one million people were killed at Auschwitz; roughly 90 percent of them Jews. In all, approximately six million Jews, in addition to another five million people the Nazis called "undesirable," were murdered.

March 9, 1945
US planes firebomb Tokyo, killing between 80,000 and 130,000 civilians.

April 30, 1945
Adolf Hitler commits suicide in Germany.

May 8, 1945
Germany surrenders. War in Europe comes to an end.

August 6, 1945
The US drops the first atomic bomb, on Hiroshima, Japan.

August 9, 1945
The US drops the second atomic bomb, on Nagasaki, Japan.

September 2, 1945
Japan formally surrenders unconditionally to allied forces aboard the battleship USS *Missouri* in Tokyo Bay.

March 5, 1946
Churchill warns of an "iron curtain" descending across Europe, identifying the Cold War that is about to dominate world events.

283

BIBLIOGRAPHY

Books

Arnold, Jennifer. *Through a Dog's Eyes*. New York: Random House, 2011.

Bausum, Ann. *Stubby the War Dog*. Washington, DC: National Geographic Children's Books, 2014.

Brooke, Geoffrey. *Singapore's Dunkirk*. London: Leo Cooper, 1989.

Daws, Gavan. *Prisoners of the Japanese*. New York: William Morrow, 1994.

Duffy, George W. *Ambushed Under the Southern Cross*. Bloomington, IN: Xlibris, 2008.

Fogle, Bruce. *The Dog's Mind*. New York: Macmillan, 1990.

George, Isabel. *The Dog that Saved My Life*. London: HarperCollins, 2010.

Hart, Ernest. *Pointers*. Neptune City, NJ: T.F.H. Publications, Inc., 1990.

Hartley, Peter. *Escape to Captivity*. London: Hamilton and Company, 1952.

Horowitz, Alexandra. *Inside of a Dog*. New York: Scribner, 2009.

Hovinga, Henk. *The Sumatra Railroad*. Leiden, Netherlands: KITLV Press, 2010.

Konstam, Angus. *Yangtze River Gunboats 1900–49*. Oxford, UK: Osprey Publishing, 2011.

Neumann, H., and E. van Witsen. *De Sumatra Spoorweg* [*The Sumatra Railway*]. Middelie, Netherlands: Studio Pieter Mulier, 1984.

Rowland, Robin. *A River Kwai Story*. Sydney, Australia: Allen and Unwin, 2008.

Varley, E. *The Judy Story*. Edited by Wendy James. London: Souvenir Press, 1973.

Wood, Alan. *The Groundnut Affair*. London: The Bodley Head, 1950.

Newspaper and Magazine Articles

Baker, Larry. "Sinbad the Four-Legged Sailor." *U.S. Coast Guard Retiree Newsletter*, July, 1988.

"Dog POW Wins Dickin Medal." *Dog World*, May 10, 1946.

"Ex-POW 'Judy' Is Dead." *Dundee Courier and Advertiser*, March 21, 1950.

Fryer, Jane. "Judy, the Dogged POW Who Defied the Japanese." *London Daily Mail*, August 12, 2010.

Howard, Philip. "Navy Will Pay Tribute to Judy the Pointer." *Times* (London), February 25, 1972.

"Judy (Ex-POW Sumatra) Is Now in England." *Tail-Wagger*, December 1945.

Locke, Michelle. "War Dogs Who Died for Our Men Finally Get Their Day." Associated Press, June 19, 1994.

"Missing, Now Safe." *Portsmouth Evening News*, May 4, 1942.

"More Help for Judy." *Tail-Wagger*, February 1946.

"Our Judy Fund." *Tail-Wagger*, April 1946.

"Presentation to Judy." *Tail-Wagger*, June 1946.

Read, Nicholas. "Prison Camp Heroine Judy was History's Only Bow-Wow POW." *Vancouver Sun*, March 12, 2003.

"Readers' Help for Judy." *Tail-Wagger*, January 1946.

Shute, Joe. "Dogs of War: The Unsung Heroes of the Trenches." *London Daily Telegraph*, October 29, 2014.

"Stubby, Hero Mascot of Seventeen Battles, Showing Decorations for Bravery." *New York Evening World*, July 8, 1921.

Turnau, Amber. "The Incredible Tale of Frank Williams." *Burnaby Now*, March 19, 2003.

Internet Articles

Putney, William W. "The War Dog Platoons: Marine Dogs of World War II." Converted from *Always Faithful: A Memoir of the Marine Dogs of WWII*. World War II History Info, worldwar2history.info/Marines/dogs.html (accessed March 21, 2014).

Backovic, Lazar. "Britain's Luftwoofe: The Heroic Paradogs of World War II." Spiegel Online, spiegel.de/international/zeitgeist/the-parachuting -dogs-of-the-british-army-in-world-war-ii-a-939002.html (accessed October 23, 2014).

"Koreans in the Imperial Japanese service." WWIIF, ww2f.com/topic/15019 -koreans-in-the-imperial-japanese-service (accessed October 27, 2014).

"The Dogs of War—A Short History of Canines in Combat." MHN: Military History Now, militaryhistorynow.com/2012/11/08/the-dogs-of-war-a -short-history-of-canines-in-combat (accessed October 29, 2014).

Websites

frankwilliams.ca

Archives

United States National Archives

"Banno, Hirateru." 8th Army Sugamo Released Prisoner 201 Files. RG 338. Folder 20, Box 4, 290/66/21/1.

Imperial War Museum

Baxter, Arthur Leonard. Oral History, IWM 13278.

Fitzgerald, J. F. Private Papers, IWM 8209.

Freeman, F. G. Private Papers, IWM 14046.

Oliver, A. C. W. Collection, IWM HU43990.

Pentney, J. D. Private Papers, IWM 20664.

Persons, J. E. R. Private Papers, IWM 18760.

Robins, J. A. C. Private Papers, IWM 5153.

Robson, Ken. Private Papers, IWM 11338.

Saddington, Stanley. Collection, IWM 2010-02-04.

Simmonds, A. B. Private Papers, IWM 21578.

Smith, W. R. Private Papers, IWM 8443.

Admiralty Files

"HMS *Truculent* Patrol Report, 12th June to 5th July, 1944," NA ADM 199/1868, Pt. 1.

General Files

"Account HMS *Dragonfly* by Comm. C. C. Alexander," NA WO 361/178.

"Singapore and Far East Personal Experiences," NA WO 106/2550.

"HMS *Grasshopper* Packet," NA WO 361/404.

"Various Reports on Sinkings of HMS *Kuala* and *Tien Kwang*," NA CO 980/237.

"Hirateru Banno and Six Others," NA CO 235/1034.

"Report of Charles Baker," NA 199/357.

"Report of R. A. Stuart of Hong Kong and Shanghai Bank," NA WO 222/1378.

"Evacuation from Singapore Across Sumatra," NA WO 141/100.

"Liberated POW Interrogation Questionnaire: Frank Williams," NA WO 344/409.

"Japanese POW Index Card: Frank Williams," NA WO 345/56.

ACKNOWLEDGMENTS

One day in the summer of 2013, I was idly flipping through the pages of *The People's Almanac*, David Wallechinsky and Irving Wallace's massive book of lists, factoids, and esoterica. As I skipped through accounts of "Great Detectives and Their Most Famous Cases" and biographies of fictional characters like Mr. Spock, my eye was caught by a brief paragraph or two concerning a dog that had become a POW during World War II.

Since that fateful day, Judy and her adventures with Frank Williams have accounted for most of my thoughts and energy. My researcher, Dr. Kevin Jones, was instrumental in scouring the archival record and helping me pursue Judy's story, which at times was hard to dig up. Without him, this book would be much the poorer (and he provided this *Raiders of the Lost Ark* fan an excuse to address someone as "Doctor Jones").

Several people helped to shed light on the mostly

forgotten POW experience in Sumatra. Henk Hovinga not only wrote a book on the subject but was quite helpful in answering my numerous follow-up questions. In the UK, historian Lizzie Oliver not only was kind enough to meet with me but pointed me to the sketches of Judy her grandfather made while held captive. I'd also like to thank Robin Rowland, Noel Tunny, and Gavan Daws.

I was fortunate to get help from any number of excellent research staffs, especially the group at the Imperial War Museum, the UK National Archives, the Portsmouth City Archives, the Southampton Government Archives, the Greenwich National Maritime Museum, and the University of Houston Libraries. Jeff Walden at the BBC Written Archives Centre was also quite helpful. Donald Degraen provided vital translations from Dutch to English. David Lambert drew the maps that appear to help guide the narrative.

I had the great honor of speaking directly with two men who not only survived Pakan Baroe (not to mention several other hellish experiences) but, as of this writing, remain alive and well—dare I say feisty. To George Duffy of New Hampshire, USA, and Rouse Voisey of Norwich, UK, I salute you, and I hope this book does justice to your experiences.

I have had the great fortune of excellent editors to

guide me, from John Parsley in the adult version of this book to Lisa Yoskowitz and Pam Garfinkel for this version. My agent, Farley Chase, was instrumental as always. My thanks as well to Reagan Arthur, Karen Landry, Shannon Langone, Heather Fain, Sabrina Callahan, Miriam Parker, and the invaluable Malin von Euler-Hogan for their help from the newly open offices of Little, Brown.

Most of all, I'd like to thank my family, especially my wife, Lorie Burnett, for their patience and loving embrace.